OSPREY COMBAT AIRCRAFT • 10

SBD DAUNTLESS
UNITS OF
WORLD WAR 2

SERIES EDITOR: TONY HOLMES

OSPREY COMBAT AIRCRAFT • 10

SBD DAUNTLESS
UNITS OF
WORLD WAR 2

Barrett Tillman

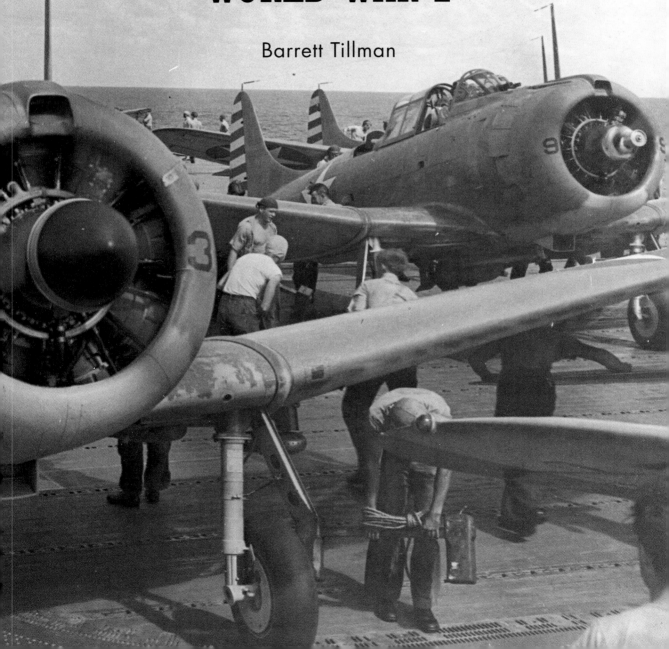

Front Cover
**Bombing Three's Lt Sid Bottomley Jr
levels out just above the tracer-
whipped sea in SBD-3 BuNo 03246
following his dive-bombing attack
on the Japanese Carrier Striking
Force on 4 June 1942. The SBD's
successful strike on Adm Nagumo's
fleet during the Battle of Midway has
since been universally recognised as
the pivotal action of the Pacific War.
Awarded a Navy Cross for his part in
this momentous sortie, Bottomley
was accompanied on the raid from
USS *Yorktown* (CV 5) by AMM2/c
Daniel F Johnson. The lieutenant
went on to see more action with
VB-3 (now aboard USS *Saratoga*
(CV 3)) during the Battle of the
Eastern Solomons on 24 August
1942, participating in the sinking of
the Japanese light carrier *Ryujo*
(*cover artwork by Iain Wyllie*)**

First published in Great Britain in 1998 by Osprey Publishing
Elms Court, Chapel Way, Botley, Oxford, OX2 9LP

© 1998 Osprey Publishing Limited

ISBN 1 85532 732 5

Edited by Tony Holmes
Page design by TT Designs, T & B Truscott
Cover Artwork by Iain Wyllie
Aircraft Profiles by Tom Tullis
Figure Artwork by Mike Chappell
Scale Drawings by Mark Styling

Origination by Valhaven Ltd, Isleworth
Printed in Hong Kong

98 99 00 01 02   10 9 8 7 6 5 4 3 2 1

EDITOR'S NOTE
To make this best-selling series as authoritative as possible, the editor would be
extremely interested in hearing from any individual who may have relevant
photographs, documentation or first-hand experiences relating to the elite
pilots, and their aircraft, of the various theatres of war. Any material used will
be fully credited to its original source. Please write to Tony Holmes at 10
Prospect Road, Sevenoaks, Kent, TN13 3UA, Great Britain.

ACKNOWLEDGMENTS
The author wishes to thank the following individuals for their assistance in the
compilation of this volume; Cdr David Cawley, Doug Champlin, Dr Steve
Ewing, John B Lundstrom, the late Gen Richard C Mangrum, Frank
McFadden, Dr Frank Olynyk, Rear Adm James D Ramage, James C Sawruk,
the late Capt Wallace C Short, Jerry Scutts, the late Capt James E Vose and
Rear Adm Edwin Wilson.

CONTENTS

THE SCOUT-BOMBING MISSION

Pearl Harbor, Coral Sea, Midway, Guadalcanal, the Marianas and the Philippines – a Pacific War 'tour guide'. All were mileposts in the combat career of the Douglas SBD Dauntless, arguably the most important naval strike aircraft of all time.

No other carrier-based attack aeroplane has exerted such a far-ranging effect on world history. At Midway alone, three SBD squadrons reversed the course of the Pacific War, whilst the Dauntless's contribution both before and after this pivotal action added greater lustre to the name.

At the time of the Pearl Harbour raid, US Navy air groups were still experiencing a period of transition. Fighting (VF) squadrons had only recently become fully equipped with monoplanes, as the last Grumman F3F-3s finally left frontline service in 1940. FitRons now flew Grumman F4F-3 Wildcats and Brewster F2A-3 Buffalos.

Torpedo (VT) units maintained the Douglas TBD-1s they had flown since 1937, although Grumman TBF-1 Avengers started to enter service in January 1942. The first fleet squadron issued with the new 'torpecker' was VT-8, who maintained a detachment nominally assigned to USS *Hornet* (CV 8). That ship's bombing and scouting units had still been flying Curtiss SBC-4 biplanes as late as December 1941, however. *Ranger* (CV 4) and *Wasp* (CV 7) had Vought SB2U-1 and -2 scout-bombers.

US Navy Bureau of Aeronautics number (BuNo) 9745 was the prototype for Northrop's BT-1 dive-bomber. First flown in 1935, it entered production with 54 examples, and saw fleet service with VB-5 and -6 from 1938. The BT-1 subsequently became the basis for the follow-on SBD-1 after the Northrop facility at El Segundo, in California, was transferred to the Douglas Aircraft Company. The design team refined the BT into a sleeker, more modern, aircraft with fully retractable landing gear, but retained the basic planform and airfoil

The generic designation VSB defined the scout-bomber mission: a dual-purpose aircraft suitable both for reconnaissance and attack. Consequently, SBDs comprised half the complement of a standard US Navy air group in late 1941. The scouting (VS) squadron nominally had 18 Dauntlesses assigned, as did the bombing (VB) squadron. Between them, they operated 36 of the 72 aircraft usually embarked, although it was not unusual for the air group commander to have a personally assigned SBD as well.

Descended from Northrop's BT-1 dive-bomber of 1935, the Douglas SBD-1 first flew at El Segundo, in California, on 1 May 1940 – just as the Battle of France entered its final phase. The US Marine Corps (USMC) received the 'dash ones' to replace ageing Great Lakes BG biplanes, while the longer-ranged SBD-2s went to Navy carrier squadrons, beginning in early 1941.

Edward H Heinemann became known as 'Mr Attack Aviation' in US military circles. He led the BT project which produced the BT-1, and remained to refine that aircraft into the SBD. Additionally, his World War 2 designs included the Douglas A-20 Havoc and A-26 Invader light bombers for the Army Air Force, and postwar he produced a long-lived series of Navy types. The latter included the piston-engined AD/A-1 Skyraider, followed by the jet-powered A3D/A-3 Skywarrior and A4D/A-4 Skyhawk. Heinemann died in 1990, widely respected by the myriad aviators who flew his aeroplanes

'VICTOR SUGAR' – SCOUTING

Three types of VS squadrons were found in the US Navy before and during World War 2. Carrier-based scouting units flew two-seat, single-engine monoplanes such as the SB2U or SBD, and later the Curtiss SB2C Helldiver. Observation-scouting (VOS) units flew two-seat, single-engine floatplanes from battleships and cruisers, largely to call naval gun-fire from their host vessels. Typically, VOS squadrons operated Curtiss SOC biplanes or Vought OS2U monoplanes. The third type of unit, also designated VS, filled the 'inshore patrol' function, flying from land bases in relatively secure areas. Their primary mission was anti-submarine

Contrary to usual practise, the US Marine Corps received the initial batch of production SBD-1s in 1940, Marine Bombing Squadron One (VMB-1) being among the earliest Dauntless units. Standard prewar markings include chrome yellow wings and vertically-striped rudder, while the LSO stripes are absent from the starboard side of the vertical fin. The squadron was redesignated VMSB-132 in July 1941 and deployed to Guadalcanal in November-December 1942, followed by a second combat tour in late 1943
(*Peter B Mersky via John Elliott*)

BuNo 1957 was only the second production Dauntless built, and it was assigned to Maj Albert Cooley, CO of VMB-1, in 1941. Red LSO stripes were only applied to the port side of the vertical stabiliser, which was visible to the landing signal officer while the aircraft approached the flight deck. Cooley remained in command of VMSB-132 until February 1942, and rose to the rank of colonel during the war. He served as assistant director of Marine Corps aviation, and was instrumental in placing Marine squadrons aboard carriers in 1944-45

patrol, either with carrier-type aircraft or OS2Us on wheels instead of floats. By 1944 nearly half the SBD squadrons outside the Continental United States were land-based VS units.

Naval aviators assigned to carrier-based VS or VB squadrons were cross-trained in both roles. It was not unusual for bombing pilots to fly scout missions, especially when the search area was wider than could be covered by 18 dedicated VS aircraft. In those instances when scouts found enemy ships, standard procedure was to send a contact report before conducting a dive-bombing attack.

The typical SBD loadout for a scouting mission was a 500-lb general-purpose bomb under the centreline rack. The larger size and heavier weight of a 1000-pounder penalised the aircraft's range and/or endurance, hence selection of the smaller weapon. Usually a pair of SBDs flew together in each search sector, not only to improve chances for a hit on an enemy ship, but to provide mutual navigation and support.

Assuming all 18 scouts were launched in pairs, they covered nine search sectors – pie-shaped 'wedges', typically 200 miles on a side with a 20- to 50-mile cross leg, before turning for 'point option', the carrier's expected position upon their return. Obviously, if more than 90 degrees were to be searched, some bombers would also be required. However, from the late summer of 1942, the long-legged TBF Avenger increasingly filled the scouting role, allowing VB aircraft to be retained for strike missions only.

Communications were a paramount concern for scouts, as immediate notification of hostile contact was crucial. SBD rear seatmen were either rated radiomen or ordnancemen, but had to be proficient both in com-

The SBD's speed brakes at full extension, with dive flaps on top and landing flaps on the bottom. The tennis ball sized holes allowed the slipstream to pass through the flaps without losing air flow over the tail surfaces, especially the elevators, thus facilitating dive recovery. This aircraft is A-24B 42-54582, which was restored to SBD-5 configuration by the author and his father in 1971-72 and flown for several years. The dive-bomber eventually joined the Marine Air-Ground Museum at Quantico, Virginia, in 1976

Saratoga Air Group turns up on the deck of CV 3 during peacetime operations in the fall of 1941. Fighting Three's F4F-3 Wildcats are spotted first for a deck-run take-off, followed by VB- and VS-3 SBD-2s and -3s, with Torpedo Three's TBD-1s ranged along the port side aft. All aircraft bear the standard Navy light grey overall colour scheme, with the national insignia containing the red ball in four positions – upper port and lower starboard wings, plus each side of the fuselage

munications and gunnery. Voice radio in 1942 was far from reliable, with a relatively short range, while clarity could be degraded by atmospheric conditions. Therefore, Morse Code was usually employed to send a contact report.

'VICTOR BAKER' – BOMBING

Bombing was the SBD's primary purpose in life – hitting a difficult target, sometimes manoeuvring at high speed in open water. The precision required to put a single bomb on a 350-ft long, 40-ft wide, destroyer turning at 30 to 35 knots was only obtained through arduous practise.

A full-scale bombing attack involved 18 SBDs approaching the target in three six-aircraft divisions. Each division was comprised of two sections, each with a leader and two wingmen flying three-aircraft vics. Usually the wingmen flew slightly behind on either side, stepped up or down according to the tactical situation.

Approaching the dive point at 14,000 to 15,000 ft, the squadron shifted from vics into echelon. At this point each pilot took interval on the Dauntless ahead of him, reduced throttle and extended the dive brakes – in the SBD, perforated flaps split at the trailing edge of the wing to slow the descent. In a standard dive-bombing approach, the aircraft descended at 70 to 75 degrees to the vertical at some 240 knots. From 'pushover' to release altitude – usually 1500 to 2000 ft – the dive took 30 to 35 seconds.

Different squadrons had variations on the standard theme, according to experience and circumstances. If fighter interception were likely, the gunners had their canopies open and .30-cal machine guns deployed.

The radioman-gunner of an SBD-3 prepares to load his right-hand M-2 Browning. The .30-06 cartridges are belted with one in four tracer, distinguished by black-tipped bullets. Combat aircrewmen were proficient both in communications and gunnery, being responsible for voice radio and Morse Code, as well as the defence of the aircraft against enemy fighters

Some squadrons stowed the guns during the dive itself, then 'unshipped' the weapons after pullout.

A fully-armed SBD on a bombing mission carried a 1000-lb general-purpose, or armour-piercing (AP), weapon under the fuselage, plus a 100-lb light bomb beneath each wing. Fusing varied according to the expected target – a heavily-armoured ship was best attacked with AP bombs fitted with delayed-action fuses to permit detonation inside the hull.

After release, the pilot retracted the dive brakes, as the SBD would not easily maintain level flight with the brakes extended. Pullout was often left as late as possible so as to reduce exposure to enemy anti-aircraft fire, and a high-speed jinking run was made to the pre-briefed rendezvous point. The 'RV' was normally in the direction of the return flight in order to expedite regrouping. A lone scout-bomber caught at low level stood little chance of surviving a determined fighter attack – safety lay in numbers, and the defence offered by multiple guns.

The SBD's well-designed controls permitted precise corrections during

Enterprise's air group commander shows off his SBD-2 with special markings on the fuselage, probably in late 1941. Note the legend 'CEG' on the wing stub as well. Holding his Dauntless nose high, with right aileron and left rudder, the 'Big E's' CAG is positioned in a slip toward the photo-aircraft. Light, positive control responses were probably the main reason for the SBD's popularity with its pilots

the dive, especially along the roll axis due to Douglas' superb ailerons. Pilots who flew the Dauntless as well as the SB2C Helldiver usually preferred the SBD as a more stable platform in a 70-degree dive at 210 knots indicated airspeed (241 mph). The SB2C-1 and -3 both indicated 310 knots (355 mph), while the improved flaps in the 'dash four' and 'five' reduced speed to about 260 knots (300 mph), often with better accuracy.

FROM SBCS TO SBDS

James E Vose was a 1934 graduate of the US Naval Academy who entered flight training in 1940. Following receipt of his wings of gold, he reported to Scouting Squadron Six (VS-6), flying Curtiss SBCs. His recollections of that period illustrate some of the problems inherent in the transition from biplanes to monoplanes;

'Scouting Six had SBC-3s when I got there, a biplane with landing gear that had to be cranked up or down – this was done with the left hand while flying close formation. We frequently would land nine planes in formation at NAS North Island (San Diego), and I can recall some hairy experiences coming over the tower as the inside man in a left turn while getting gear and flaps down!

'In 1941 a group of us were sent to the Douglas plant at El Segundo for checkouts in the plane, and then back to the squadron. I left VS-6, along with others, in November 1941 to form Bombing Eight in the *Hornet* at Norfolk, Virginia.

'On arrival at East Field, Norfolk, we "red hot" SBD pilots found that our planes in VB-8 were SBC-4s, which had two distinctive attributes. The wheels and flaps did not have to be hand cranked, and when the prop was put into full low pitch it became the noisiest plane extant!

'I believe that in March 1942 we left Norfolk for San Diego, turned in the SBC-4s, and received SBD-3s. Then to San Francisco to pick up the Doolittle group, and off to their launching. The B-25s being launched, several of the more experienced pilots were sent on a search. I and one other pilot were the only ones that had landed an SBD on a carrier. All but one plane got aboard, which is some kind of record when the existing weather and degree of training are considered. The SBD was an honest airplane.'

The attack on Pearl extended the SBD's life well beyond that envisioned by the Navy. A batch of 174 SBD-3s had been ordered in September 1940, with delivery commencing in March 1941. The final aircraft of this order was accepted in January 1942, by which time an available obsolescent SBD was worth infinitely more than a bigger, faster, unavailable SB2C Helldiver (see *Osprey Combat Aircraft 3 - Helldiver Units of World War 2*, also by Barrett Tillman, for further details). In March 1942 El Segundo began turning out hundreds of additional SBDs and Army A-24s, this process continuing unabated for the next 28 months.

Meanwhile, operational squadrons were suddenly faced with the challenge of adapting – literally overnight – from a peacetime stance to sudden combat. That sometimes difficult transition was explained by retired Cdr Harold L Buell, a highly-experienced dive-bomber pilot who subsequently earned a doctorate in history;

'When we began wartime carrier operations in 1942, there was a mass of "squadron operational procedures", both on the carriers and within the

Transitional markings are evident on these six SBD-2s in 1941. They have received blue-grey upper surfaces and medium grey under surfaces, with a single white LSO chevron on the tail. They are most likely from one of the two *Enterprise* SBD squadrons, VB- or VS-6, although the side numbers are absent. It is possible that the naval censor had removed the identifying marks as a security measure by the time this photo was released to the public

In near identical colours to the previous echelon photo, these Scouting Six SBDs approach *Enterprise* on Navy Day, 27 October 1941. One year later 'The Big E' and her Dauntlesses would be heavily engaged in the Battle of Santa Cruz, in which the ship suffered heavy damage from Japanese carrier aircraft

air groups, that simply did not work in a wartime reality. Changes began immediately, and were continuous as new ways of doing things better were tried. I am not sure that much of this change ever got written down per se, but was spread more or less by word of mouth between groups and their carriers.

'Some "old timers" in both places were more reluctant than others to change the book and try better things – hence there were different levels of capability in our ships and squadrons. For example, a John Crommelin-type of thinker as "air boss" could have a tremendous impact upon both his ship and the embarked group, and the "Big E", and squadrons under his leadership, emerged as superior in combat. Take a close look at the records of the *Enterprise* and some other carriers in 1942 and you can see what I mean – it was not all just a matter of luck! As a young junior officer at that time, I simply kept my eyes and ears open and my mouth shut, thus learning the right way of doing things. After all, surviving – living or dying – was involved in it all!'

One of the most experienced SBD pilots of the 1941-42 period was Lt James M 'Moe' Vose, who had joined Hornet Air Group as a Curtiss SBC pilot before Bombing Eight received SBD-2s. Vose flew at Midway and Santa Cruz, then returned to combat in 1943 as commanding officer of VB-17, the first SB2C Helldiver squadron to be formed, and see action

EARLY COMBAT

When Japan attacked the Territory of Hawaii on 7 December 1941, eight US Navy and two USMC squadrons were equipped with SBDs. All but two of the carrier-based SBD units were assigned to the Pacific Fleet, as *Lexington* (CV 2), *Saratoga* (CV 3) and *Enterprise* (CV 6) operated from Pearl Harbour, Hawaii or San Diego, in California. *Yorktown* (CV 5), on the Atlantic coast, was immediately rushed to the Pacific, leaving *Ranger* (CV 4) and *Wasp* (CV 7) operating SB2U-1s and -2s, while the new *Hornet* (CV 8) was still fitting out with SBC-4s.

SBD Squadrons – December 1941

VB-2	16 SBD-2	USS *Lexington* (CV 2)
VS-2	18 SBD-2/3	USS *Lexington* (CV 2)
VB-3	21 SBD-3	USS *Saratoga* (CV 3)
VS-3	22 SBD-3	USS *Saratoga* (CV 3)
VB-5	19 SBD-3	USS *Yorktown* (CV 5)
VS-5	19 SBD-3	USS *Yorktown* (CV 5)
VB-6	18 SBD-2	USS *Enterprise* (CV 6)
VS-6	18 SBD-2/3	USS *Enterprise* (CV 6)
VMSB-132	19 SBD-1	Quantico, Virginia
VMSB-232	22 SBD-1/2	Ewa, Hawaii

Total - 192

'PEARL'

The Dauntless was one of the few American aircraft in combat from the first day of the Pacific War to the last. On the morning of 7 December 1941, after delivering USMC F4Fs to Wake Island, *Enterprise* launched 18 SBD-2s and -3s on a sector search from a point 75 miles southwest of Kaula, in the Hawaiian Islands. Operating on a war footing since 28 November, Vice Adm William F Halsey's Task Force 8 was taking no chances. In two-aircraft sections, the Dauntlesses (13 scouts, 4 bombers, and the air group commander) would search nine sectors from northeast to east-southeast before 'The Big E', and her screen, returned to 'Pearl'.

West of 'Pearl' itself, Lt Cdr Howard Young and his wingman, Ens Perry L Teaff, noticed a squadron-sized formation over the USMC facility at Ewa. Shortly thereafter, one of the single-engine aircraft broke off and approached *Enterprise's* CAG section, drawing within 75 ft of Ens Teaff's tail. Teaff assumed the stranger was a playful US Army pilot, but when 7.7 mm rounds blistered the SBD's skin, the awful reality emerged as anti-aircraft gunners began shooting at any airborne aircraft. War had come to Hawaii.

Following doctrine, Teaff and Young remained together, fending off subsequent gunnery passes by the A6M2 pilot. Most of the return fire was delivered by Teaff's gunner, RM3/c E P Jinks, in 6-S-2, and the Zero

This deckload of *Enterprise* SBD-2s and -3s demonstrates the hectic transition period in naval aircraft markings following Pearl Harbor. Most Dauntlesses show the red and white striped rudders of early 1942, although a few have had the stripes obliterated with dark blue paint. Of more interest is the mixture of large and small national insignia, now carried top and bottom of both wings – some aircraft with small-diameter stars, some maximum-chord diameter overlapping the ailerons, and at least one (B-3) with one each!

Non-standard markings are evident on these *Enterprise* aircraft – largely VS-6 SBD-3s and VB-6 'dash twos'. The nearest scout – 'Sail Four' – has its fuselage star painted out, while other SBDs show either the previous small emblem or the more recent oversize wartime markings. Another erratic aspect of 'Big E' markings was the simultaneous appearance of a full-chord single LSO stripe and the shorter dual stripe, as on 'Baker Nine'. The Dauntlesses at the front of the 'pack' carry only centreline bombs, while the following SBDs, with more deck space, are also armed with 100-lb weapons beneath their wings

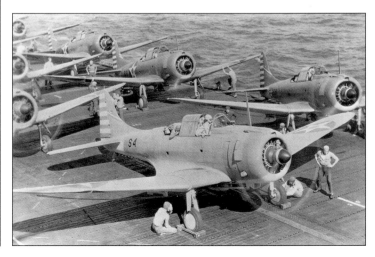

soon left to seek other sport. CAG Young and his wingman survived both the Japanese and 'friendly' American ground fire to land at Ford Island in 'Pearl'.

Others were not so fortunate. Shortly before the air group commander encountered the Japanese, *Enterprise's* radio watch heard frantic calls from Ens Manuel Gonzalez. He broadcast, 'This is 6-B-3, an American plane. Do not shoot!' Evidently attacked by Aichi D3A2s from *Shokaku* and *Zuikaku*, Gonzalez was shot down and called to his gunner to deploy their life raft, but neither he nor RM3/c Leonard Kozelek were seen again.

Ens John H Vogt Jr and RM3/c Sidney Pierce became separated from their skipper, Lt Cdr Hallstead Hopping. The wreckage of 6-S-3 was found near Ewa, apparently having collided with a Zero – there were no survivors.

Scouting Six also lost both aircraft of the seventh sector team, flown by Lt Clarence E Dickinson and Ens John R McCarthy. Concerned about flak, bomb explosions and dense smoke in the area, the team scouted Barbers Point trying to make sense of the chaos. They were jumped by A6Ms at 4000 ft and had little chance – McCarthy bailed out at only 200 ft and broke a leg on landing. Dickinson was swarmed by five fighters, and although he returned fire his Dauntless was set ablaze. He too parachuted to safety, but both radioman-gunners were killed.

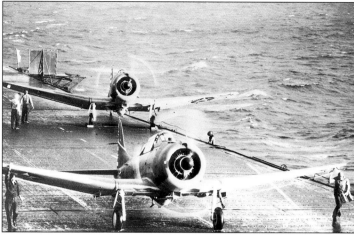

Likewise, Lt(jg) Frank Patriarca's team was intercepted and his wingman, Ens Walter Willis, disappeared near Oahu's south coast with Chief FJ Ducolon in the back seat.

Another *Enterprise* team nearly reached safety, only to encounter the Army's manic, undisciplined, ground fire. Passing Fort Weaver, both Dauntlesses were shot up by automatic weapons. Ens Edward T Deacon of VS-6 and his gunner were both wounded and, when their engine seized, they safely ditched offshore. Their VB-6 partner, Ens Wilbur E Roberts, landed a perforated Dauntless at Hickam Field.

Five SBDs had been shot down by Japanese aircraft and one by American gunners. Three pilots and five rear seat men were dead, with two other pilots and a radioman injured. Of the surviving 13 SBDs, 10 were available at Ford Island, where Lt Cdr Hopping organised an impromptu search to the north. They scoured the sea for three hours without result, as the Japanese carrier striking force had departed to the northwest.

The men who flew into Pearl on 7 December faced a long war of attrition. Four more pilots and five radiomen were lost in operations during 1942, including Lt Cdr Hopping, while one crew was captured at Marcus Island and two more men were wounded. In all, the 36 fliers who left 'The Big E' that Sunday morning sustained 17 killed and 7 wounded or cap-

Loaded with 500-lb bombs, these SBD-3s stand ready for take-off in early 1942. Even in heavy weather, and with rain making the carrier deck slippery, wartime operations proceeded on schedule

Bombing Six prepares to launch on one of four missions flown during the Gilbert Islands raid of 1 February 1942. *Enterprise's* first strike involved 36 SBDs in a pre-dawn launch against Kwajalein Atoll, while the second and third SBD missions involved 13 and 9 sorties, respectively, against Taroa Island. The last mission committed eight SBDs against Wotje Atoll. Losses during the day amounted to six aircraft, including five SBDs, from 66 strike sorties. Three Dauntlesses were shot down by Mitsubishi A5M fighters, partly owing to an insufficient number of F4F Wildcats being made available for escort duties

tured – a 75 per cent casualty rate throughout the war.

HIT AND RUN

In February and March 1942 the Pacific Fleet carriers conducted a series of hit-and-run raids against Japanese-held islands, including a 'double header' in the Gilberts and Marshalls on Sunday, 1 February.

Before dawn Enterprise Air Group launched behind CAG Howard Young, who had flown into the Pearl surprise 58 days before. Primary targets for Vice Adm Halsey's task force were Roi and Kwajalein Atolls, with VS-6 sent against the former. The CO, Lt Cdr

Halstead Hopping, led his Dauntlesses down on the enemy airfield and its alert defenders. Hopping had just dropped when his SBD-3 was attacked from below by a nimble Mitsubishi A5M (later 'Claude'), which shot him into the water. Fighters downed another SBD, while two other scouts also were lost for negligible damage to the base.

At Kwajalein, VB-6 flew three missions, partly against the air base that had supported bombing missions against the US Marines on Wake Island. Employing mainly 500- and 100-lb bombs, Lt Cdr W R Hollingsworth's pilots first attacked the light cruiser *Katori*, then returned to strike at the airfield's hangars. Ens Doherty and AOM3/c W E Hunt succumbed to defending fighters, but the executive officer, Lt Richard H Best (formerly of VF-2), out-flew a pair of A5Ms that holed his SBD's tail. Ever the objective professional, Best concluded, 'They didn't use enough deflection on me!'

Withdrawing from the area, *Enterprise* was attacked by five Mitsubishi G4M land-attack bombers, one of which attempted to crash onto the carrier's deck. The 'Big E's' manoeuvring, coupled with courageous action by AMM Bruno Gaido, who manned a parked SBD's free machine gun, resulted in a very near miss. One of the bomber's wings severed the tail of

On 1 February – the same day that Vice Adm W F Halsey's *Enterprise* task force struck the Gilberts – Rear Adm F J Fletcher's *Yorktown* group attacked other targets in the Gilberts and Marshalls. Eight aircraft were lost mainly to poor weather and fuel exhaustion in operations over Jaluit, Makin and Mili, in exchange for little damage inflicted upon the enemy. Following the command 'Prepare for launching planes', *Yorktown's* 'roof' swarms with deckcrew, removing chocks and tie-down lashings, as the carrier turns into wind on 1 February

Two of *Yorktown's* leading lights were Lt Cdrs William O Burch of VS-5 and Joseph Taylor of VT-5. They led their respective squadrons in the hit-and-run raids against the Gilberts, Marshalls and New Guinea during February and March 1942, then in May fought in the Battle of the Coral Sea and helped sink the Japanese light carrier *Shoho* (*Naval Aviation Museum*)

Despite non-folding wings, the SBD's 41-ft span fit with room to spare on a standard carrier elevator. This aircraft is Bombing Six's B-3, and is seen on its way from *Enterprise's* hangar deck up to the flight deck, where it will be spotted for launch against Wake Island on 24 February 1942. The plane captain rides in the pilot's seat to operate the brakes, while handlers prepare to push the Dauntless into position prior to launch

Gaido's SBD, spread burning gasoline across the deck and splashed overboard. Gaido was subsequently promoted and assigned as aircrew on the basis of demonstrated competence!

Meanwhile, Rear Adm Frank Jack Fletcher's *Yorktown* group sought targets in the Gilberts. Again, the raiders inflicted minor damage for heavy loss – eight aircraft failed to return, although most may have ditched having exhausted their fuel supplies. CAG, Cdr C S Smiley, led 16 VB-5 crews against Jaluit, finding almost no opposition, but atrocious weather, with dangerously low ceilings. Lt Cdr William O Burch Jr took nine of his VS-5 scouts to Makin, while his XO, Lt Wallace C Short, led five more to nearby Mili. Burch's flight destroyed two moored flying boats, but Short's group came up empty handed. Some SBDs barely managed a safe return with as little as two gallons remaining.

Enterprise was back in action on 24 February, striking Japan's newly-conquered Wake Island. VB-6 bombed the airfield and sank a pair of flying boats in the lagoon, but the scouts lost an SBD to AA fire. A

Deckcrewmen check that the 500-pounder they have just secured to the bomb crutch has been mounted correctly. Prior to the bomb being hoisted up into the cradle by a hand-winch, squadron armourers would set the weapon's fuse for either delayed or impact detonation

subsequent raid on Marcus Island on 4 March was similarly disappointing. Arriving early over the target owing to a tailwind, the SBDs bombed by flare and moonlight, but low clouds interfered. Buildings and runways were targeted, with a VS-6 aircraft lost to flak.

America's first two-carrier operation of the war occurred on 10 March when *Lexington* and *Yorktown* teamed up to hit Lae and Salamaua, in New Guinea. The two carriers put up an impressive 104 aircraft, launching only 45 miles off the southern coast. Overflying the Papua Peninsula, the carrier avia-

Marked 'GC', the SBD-3 of Cdr Howard Young is first off the deck of *Enterprise* as the air group commander leads the first strike against Wake Island. At this point the former American outpost had been under Japanese control for just 60 days, but it would be attacked repeatedly by US carrier aircraft for the duration of the war. Cdr Young perished in a crash not long after this photograph was taken

Tokyo bound in the distance, USS *Hornet* (CV 8), with USAAF B-25 Mitchells on board, is trailed by *Enterprise*, which embarked her own VS-6 and *Saratoga's* VB-3 for the brief foray into Japanese waters during mid-April 1942. Hornet Air Group only flew uneventful combat air patrols and anti-submarine missions on the return trip to Pearl Harbor. The group's inauguration to genuine combat came less than two months later at Midway

tors sought a way through the 13,000-ft Owen Stanley Mountain Range. *Lexington's* CAG, Cdr William B Ault, flew his SBD up the Lakekamu River, orbiting in a 7000-ft gorge to provide radio information to the strike force.

It was a successful operation, and despite poor torpedo performance, SBDs and TBDs sank three transports and damaged several other ships. The one loss was a Scouting Two SBD and crew, downed by AA fire.

Although necessarily limited in scope, these early raids provided the first generation of combat carrier aviators with much-needed experience, and a chance to evaluate their equipment. It was valuable information, that shortly would be put to good use.

COLOUR PLATES

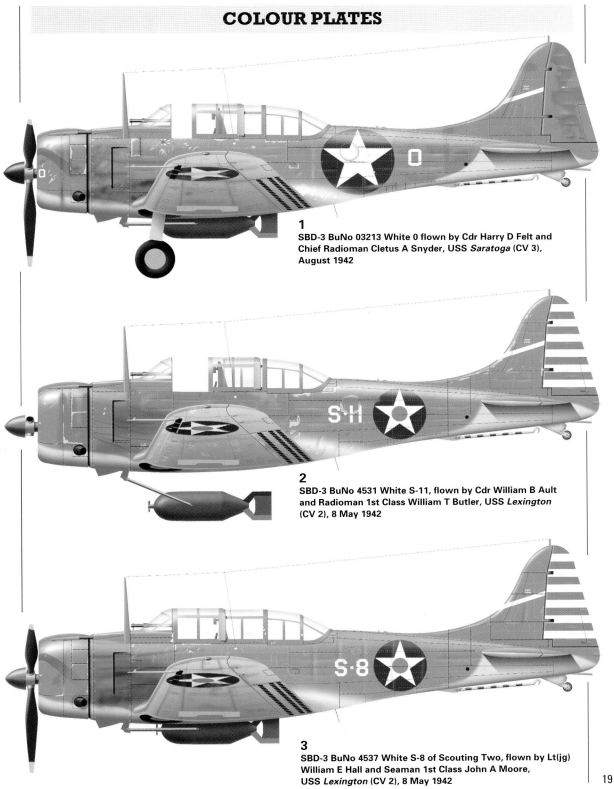

1
SBD-3 BuNo 03213 White 0 flown by Cdr Harry D Felt and
Chief Radioman Cletus A Snyder, USS *Saratoga* (CV 3),
August 1942

2
SBD-3 BuNo 4531 White S-11, flown by Cdr William B Ault
and Radioman 1st Class William T Butler, USS *Lexington*
(CV 2), 8 May 1942

3
SBD-3 BuNo 4537 White S-8 of Scouting Two, flown by Lt(jg)
William E Hall and Seaman 1st Class John A Moore,
USS *Lexington* (CV 2), 8 May 1942

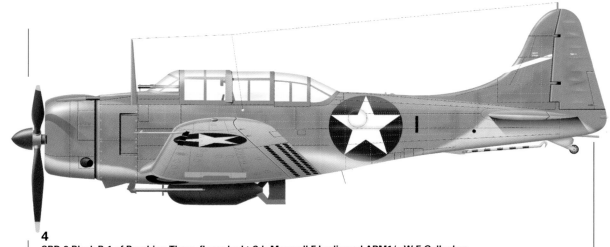

4
SBD-3 Black B-1 of Bombing Three, flown by Lt Cdr Maxwell F Leslie and ARM1/c W E Gallagher, USS *Yorktown* (CV 5), 4 June 1942

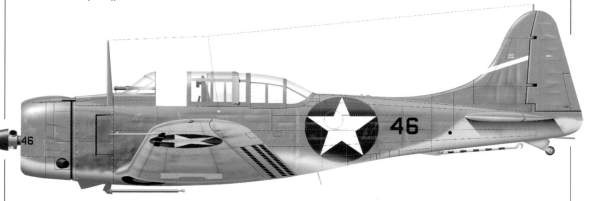

5
SBD-3 Black B-46 of Bombing Three, flown by Lt(jg) Robert M Elder and Radioman 2nd Class L A Till, USS *Saratoga* (CV 3), 24 August 1942

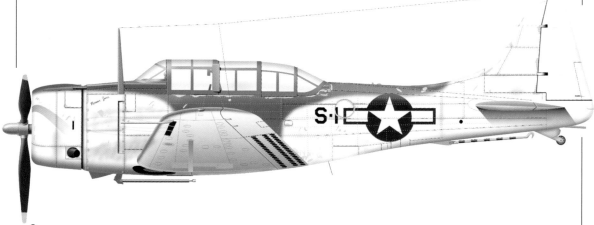

6
SBD-5 Black S-1 of VMS-3, flown by Maj Christian C Lee, US Virgin Islands, May 1944

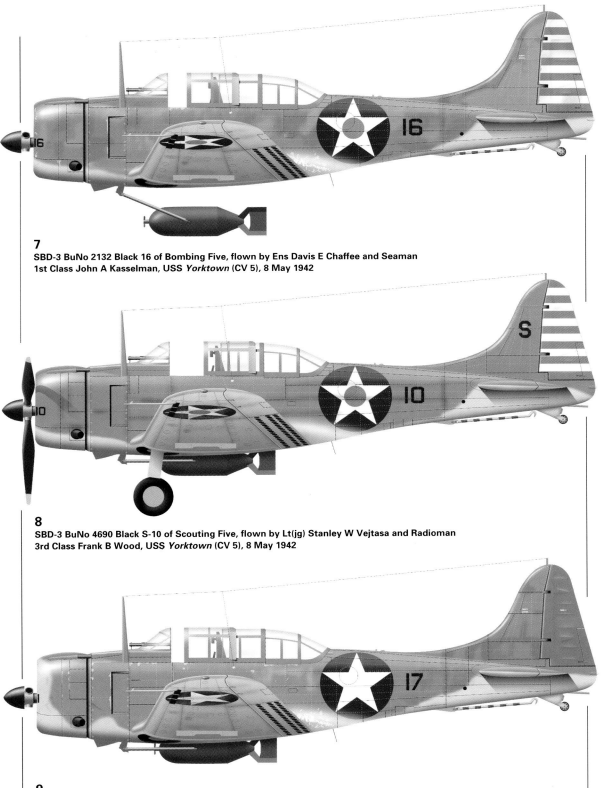

7
SBD-3 BuNo 2132 Black 16 of Bombing Five, flown by Ens Davis E Chaffee and Seaman
1st Class John A Kasselman, USS *Yorktown* (CV 5), 8 May 1942

8
SBD-3 BuNo 4690 Black S-10 of Scouting Five, flown by Lt(jg) Stanley W Vejtasa and Radioman
3rd Class Frank B Wood, USS *Yorktown* (CV 5), 8 May 1942

9
SBD-3 Black 17 of Scouting Five, flown by Ens Leif Larsen and Radioman John F Gardner,
USS *Yorktown* (CV 5), June 1942

10
SBD-3 BuNo 4687 Black B-1 of Bombing Six, flown by Lt Richard H Best
and Chief Radioman James F Murray, USS *Enterprise* (CV 6), 4 June 1942

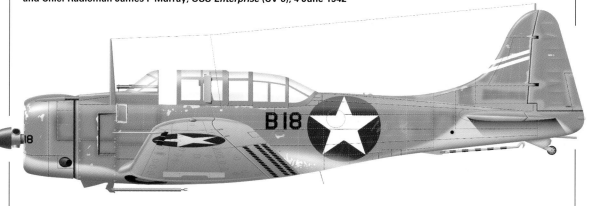

11
SBD-3 Black B-18 of Bombing Six, flown by Ens Robert C Shaw and
AO2/c Harold L Jones, USS *Enterprise* (CV 6), 8 August 1942

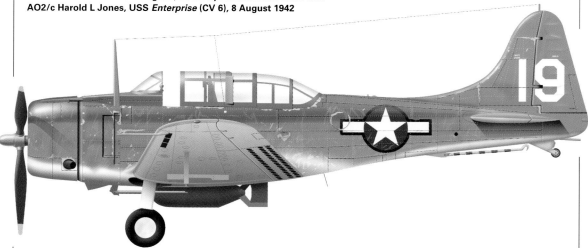

12
SBD-5 White 19 of VB-9, USS *Essex* (CV 9), early 1944

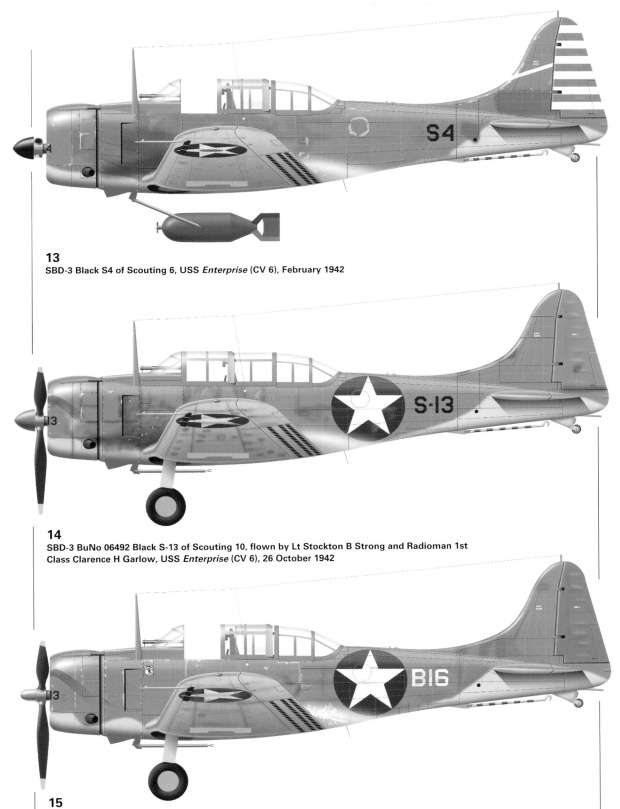

13
SBD-3 Black S4 of Scouting 6, USS *Enterprise* (CV 6), February 1942

14
SBD-3 BuNo 06492 Black S-13 of Scouting 10, flown by Lt Stockton B Strong and Radioman 1st
Class Clarence H Garlow, USS *Enterprise* (CV 6), 26 October 1942

15
SBD-3 White B16 of Bombing 11, flown by Lt(jg) Edwin Wilson and Radioman 2nd Class Harry Jespersen,
Guadalcanal, summer 1943

23

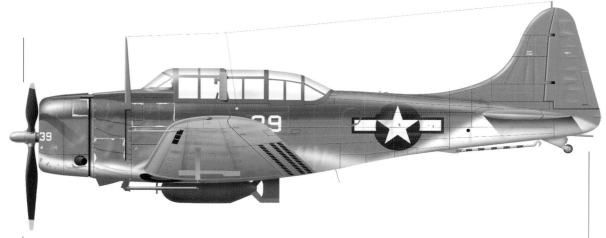

16
SBD-5 White 39 of Bombing 16, flown by Lt Cook Cleland and Radioman 2nd Class William J Hisler,
USS *Lexington* (CV 16), June 1944

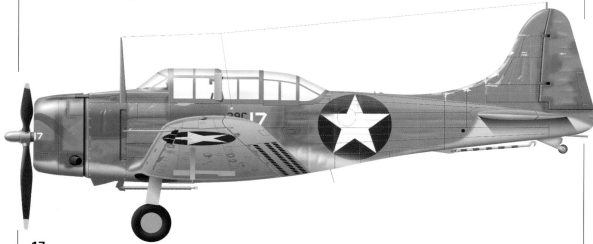

17
Douglas SBD-5 White 17 of Composite Squadron 29, USS *Santee* (CVE 29), North Atlantic, 1943

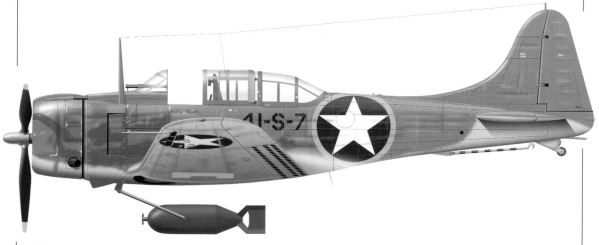

18
SBD-3 Black 41-S-7 of Scouting 41, USS *Ranger* (CV 4), November 1942

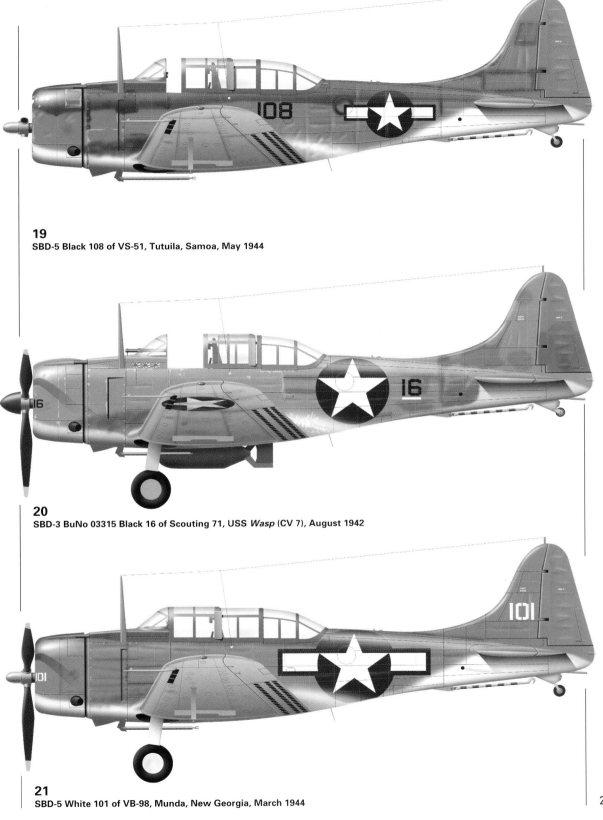

19
SBD-5 Black 108 of VS-51, Tutuila, Samoa, May 1944

20
SBD-3 BuNo 03315 Black 16 of Scouting 71, USS *Wasp* (CV 7), August 1942

21
SBD-5 White 101 of VB-98, Munda, New Georgia, March 1944

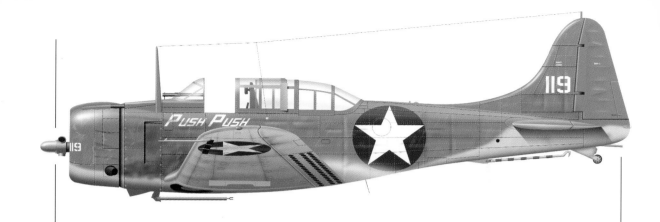

22
SBD-4/5 White 119 of VMSB-144, flown by Maj Frank E Hollar, Solomon Islands, November 1943

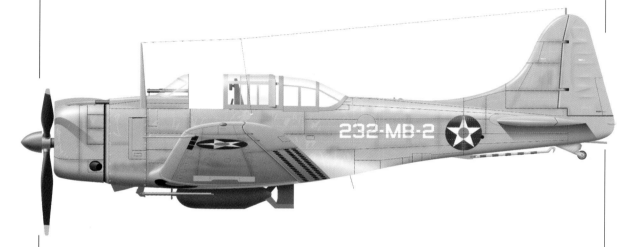

23
SBD-1 White 232-MB-2 of VMSB-232, MCAS Ewa, Territory of Hawaii, 7 December 1941

24
SBD-5 White 1 of VMSB-231, flown by Maj Elmer Glidden and M/Sgt James Boyle, Marshall Islands, 1944

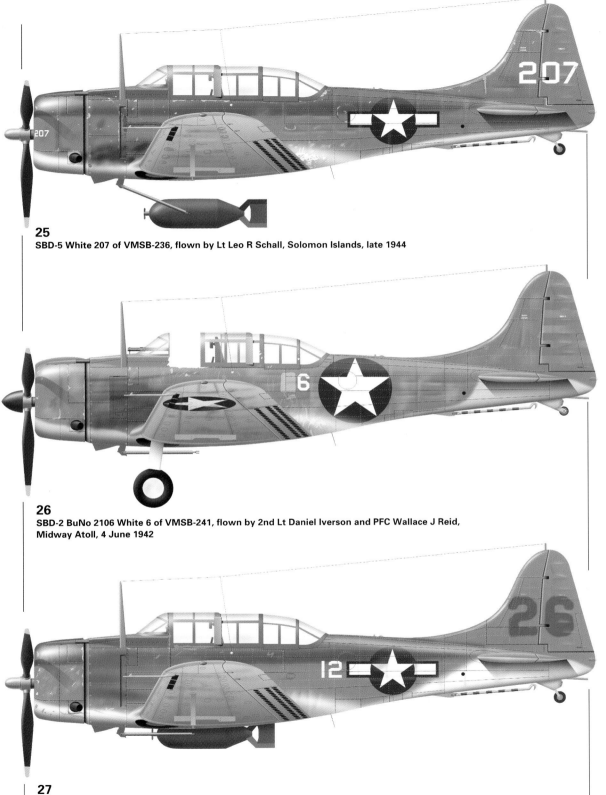

25
SBD-5 White 207 of VMSB-236, flown by Lt Leo R Schall, Solomon Islands, late 1944

26
SBD-2 BuNo 2106 White 6 of VMSB-241, flown by 2nd Lt Daniel Iverson and PFC Wallace J Reid,
Midway Atoll, 4 June 1942

27
SBD-5 White 12 of VMSB-331, Majuro Atoll, June 1944

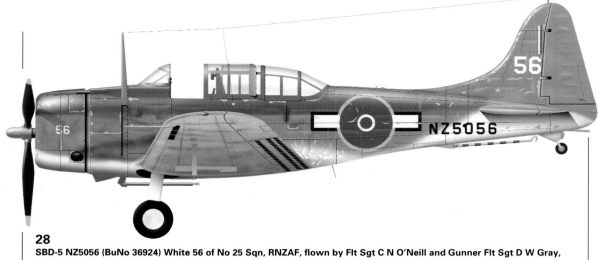

28
SBD-5 NZ5056 (BuNo 36924) White 56 of No 25 Sqn, RNZAF, flown by Flt Sgt C N O'Neill and Gunner Flt Sgt D W Gray, Piva Field, Solomons, April 1944

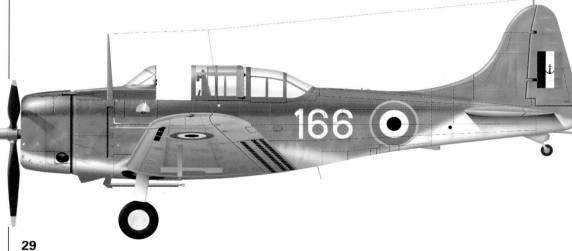

29
SBD-5 of *Flotille* 4FB, *Aeronautique Navale*, southern France, late 1944

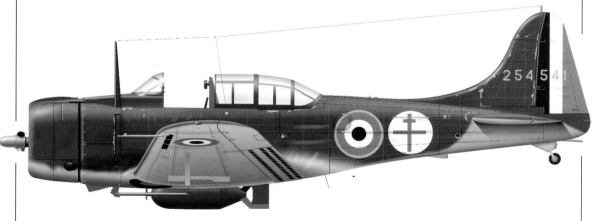

30
A-24B of *Groupe de Combat* I/18 'Vendee,' France, late 1944

1
Maj Elmer G 'Iron Man' Glidden,
CO of VMSB-231, Majuro Atoll
(Central Pacific), June 1944

2
Lt James M 'Moe' Vose, VB-8,
USS *Hornet* (CV 8), Solomon Islands,
October 1942

3
Lt James D 'Jig Dog' Ramage, VB-10,
USS *Enterprise* (CV 6), Central Pacific,
late 1943

CORAL SEA AND MIDWAY

In May and June 1942 the American and Japanese navies clashed in the first two aircraft carrier engagements of history. From the US perspective, both were battles of strategic defence, with the objective of preventing enemy seizure of Port Moresby, in New Guinea, and Midway Atoll, respectively. Twenty years of experimentation, technical advancement and doctrinal development lay behind both navies' endeavours.

CORAL SEA

The Japanese plan for the occupation of Port Moresby involved two carrier groups – light carrier *Shoho* supporting the invasion force, and Pearl Harbour veterans *Shokaku* and *Zuikaku* operating as the strike force. Enemy occupation of Port Moresby would emperil northern Australia, which was viewed as an unacceptable situation from the Allied viewpoint. Therefore, the US Pacific Fleet, still bereft of battleships, committed *Lexington* and *Yorktown* to turn back the Japanese thrust southward.

Skipper of *Yorktown's* Scouting Five (VS-5) was Lt Cdr William O Burch, who led three strikes against the Japanese anchorage at Tulagi on 4 May. *Yorktown's* flight deck crews were so efficient that the 'turnaround

Taken aboard *Yorktown* just three days before the Battle of the Coral Sea, this photo shows an SBD being guided onto an outrigger positioned off to the side of the flight deck. By parking the Dauntless in such a fashion, more aircraft could be stored on the flight deck

IJNS *Shokaku* comes under attack from Lexington and Yorktown Air Groups in the Coral Sea on 8 May 1942. SBDs obtained four hits on the 20,000-ton carrier, which sustained damage that could not be repaired in time for it to participate in the Midway operation some 30 days later. In turn, her squadrons and *Zuikaku's* sank *Lexington* and damaged *Yorktown*

Lt Wallace C Short (left front) was CO of VB-5 aboard *Yorktown* (CV 5) at Coral Sea and Midway. Bombing Five participated in attacks on Japanese carriers on 7-8 May at Coral Sea, and was the only *Yorktown* squadron to remain aboard for Midway. To avoid confusion with VB-3, which relieved VS-5 for the short Midway cruise, Short's squadron was temporarily redesignated 'Scouting Five' – a misnomer that has caused confusion among naval historians for half a century

time' prevented Burch from getting a cup of coffee after reporting to Capt Buckmaster after the first mission. Cargo ships and a destroyer were sunk in this operation.

Three days later, on the 7th, Burch led Scouting Five in the first attack against a Japanese aircraft carrier. Between them, the *Yorktown* and *Lexington* air groups put up 93 aircraft, which overwhelmed the defences of light carrier *Shoho* in the Coral Sea. As Burch related;

'One of our scouts reported that he had sighted two cruisers and two destroyers. We launched the air group. An Army plane picked up another force which had a carrier in it. While we were on the way out, I got his last word from the *Yorktown* stating that about 50 miles from our first position we would find a carrier. I think we would have seen it anyway – it was almost on our track to the other force.

'The *Lexington* group made their dive-bomb attack just ahead of me. I watched them attack – I thought it was all of their bombing group. The Jap carrier was manoeuvring heavily, and I saw only one hit. The carrier then turned into the wind to launch her planes. I immediately called Lt Cdr Joe Taylor with our torpedo planes and told him we were going in. He asked me to wait because it would be at least five minutes before he could arrive. I told him I wasn't going to wait because the carrier was launching planes and I wasn't going to let them get off.

'I got a hit and I don't think any of the squadrons behind me missed. We really laid the bombs in that day.' Postwar evaluation indicated that *Shoho* absorbed as many as 13 bombs and seven torpedoes.

'On 8 May we made contact again. The *Yorktown* group was launched first. We headed to the north about 180 miles and found the Japs. There were two carriers in the open. Just south of the Japanese task force was a large area of bad weather. They were heading for it. We co-ordinated our dive bombing and torpedo attack on the after carrier (*Shokaku*).

31

'At 8000 ft that day everything fogged up (sights and windscreen) – everybody bombed from memory. It is not a good method!

'We released at about 1500 ft. We'd pull out and be clear at 1000. We usually dive at an angle around 75 to 80 degrees and 200 to 210 knots. I always try to get as steep as I can, because the squadron has a tendency to flatten out . . . the rear planes push over a little too soon to keep track of the man ahead. Our sights are set so that, in a 70-degree dive, you put your pipper right on the target, without any wind. With practice, you get so you can judge pretty close what angle you're diving at.

'After we returned to the ship, I had only three or four planes that could go right back, and Wally Short of Bombing Five had only one or two. We were pretty well shot up from the fighters. The *Lexington* was in trouble, and the admiral decided to keep us there to protect the *Lexington* and its force. We did not go back the second time.'

Initial US claims were six bomb and three torpedo hits on *Shokaku*, but Japanese damage reports showed three bombs and no torpedoes. Burch continued;

'During seven attacks by Bombing and Scouting Five there was only one man lost from anti-aircraft fire. He was Jo-Jo Powers (Lt John J Powers), who always went way down low before pulling out. We don't know whether he was hit by AA or just went so low to make sure of a hit that his plane was hit by his own bomb fragments. Before he took off he said he was "going to lay his bomb on that Jap so-and-so's deck". They've awarded him the Medal of Honor. He deserves it.'

One of the most popular pilots of VB-5 was Lt John J Powers, a New Yorker who received a posthumous Medal of Honor for his sacrifice at Coral Sea. Known for his low-level releases, Powers advocated a minimal drop altitude in order to improve prospects for a hit. His SBD was badly hit by fighters and flak during the 8 May attack on *Shokaku*, but Powers pressed the attack home regardless, putting his half-ton bomb on target seconds before crashing into the sea with his gunner, Radioman 2nd Class Everett C Hill

'Lady Lex' in her death throes. On 8 May *Lexington* succumbed to torpedo damage inflicted by Nakajima B5Ns, which eventually ignited gasoline fumes. The attack is still in progress, as flak bursts and spray appear off the ship's port bow. During this combat, *Lexington* and *Yorktown* SBDs attempted to repel the torpedo attack, but sustained heavy losses – eight aircraft with eleven pilots or gunners in exchange for six Japanese aircraft shot down (*Tailhook Association*)

Among *Lexington's* defenders was Lt(jg) William E Hall of Scouting Two, who was awarded the Medal of Honor for his valiant part in the anti-torpedo aircraft patrol of 8 May. Although badly wounded in one foot, Hall remained in the low-level combat against Japanese attackers and succeeded in landing his battered aircraft aboard *Lexington*. He is seen here receiving his nation's highest decoration from Rear Adm John Towers

Powers' gunner was Radioman 2/c E C Hill, who was killed with his pilot in one of the classic dive bombing actions of the war.

Four SBDs were lost from the American strike, including three from *Lexington's* CAG section. The air group commander, William B Ault, was a 43-year-old professional from the Annapolis class of 1922 – probably the senior naval aviator on flight status. He radioed that he and his gunner, ARM1/c W T Butler, were wounded but claimed a hit on *Shokaku*. Only one of his wingmen returned to the ship.

The second Medal of Honour awarded to an SBD pilot went to Lt(jg) William E Hall of Scouting Two. The Japanese strike that followed the US attack on *Shokaku* involved Nakajima B5N2 torpedo aircraft, and 23 Dauntlesses were deployed at 800 to 900 ft to stop them. This procedure had been anticipated before the war, but US intelligence had no knowledge of the speedy 'Kate'.

Inbound were 18 B5Ns with 9 A6M2 Zeros – near identical numbers of US and Japanese aircraft, although initiative and performance heavily favoured the Japanese air groups. Additionally, three of the *Lexington* scouts were deployed on the unengaged starboard side, further reducing the American capability.

The confused low-level combat quickly resolved itself in favour of the attackers, for six SBDs were shot down and two more were jettisoned from *Lexington* with battle damage. Five pilots and six gunners were lost in the defence of the task force, although 'Lex' took two torpedoes and *Yorktown* two bombs. In return, the Dauntless crews claimed 17 shootdowns, including six Zeros. Their actual tally – still commendable under the circumstances – was five B5Ns and one Aichi dive-bomber.

Hall and his gunner, Seaman 1st Class John Moore, shot down a 'Kate' despite the storm of flak from US ships. They were then attacked by three Zeros, one of which put a 20 mm shell into the SBD's cockpit. Hall's right foot was nearly severed, but he remained in the fight, compensating with his left foot and trim tabs. Upon landing aboard the damaged *Lexington* his 2-S-8 was shoved overboard.

Another VS-2 crew was close by Hall's action, Ens John Leppla and Radioman John Liska in 2-S-12 claiming four A6Ms in this mission, although none were lost to SBDs. Credited with four kills in two days, Leppla was quickly identified as fighter material, only to die in his first F4F Wildcat mission with VF-10 at Santa Cruz. Leppla became the Navy's top-scoring SBD pilot with four credited victories.

Lexington succumbed to internal gasoline explosions later that day, and the battered *Yorktown* steamed for 'Pearl'. The next carrier duel was less than 30 days off.

Coral Sea Medals of Honor

Lt(jg) William E Hall

Born: 31 October 1913, Storrs, Utah

Entered Service At: Utah

Place and Date: Coral Sea, May 7-8 1942

Citation: 'For extreme courage and conspicuous heroism in combat above and beyond the call of duty as pilot of a scouting plane in action against enemy Japanese forces in the Coral Sea on May 7 and 8, 1942. In a resolute and determined attack on May 7, Lt(jg) Hall dived his plane at an enemy Japanese aircraft carrier, contributing materially to the destruction of that vessel. On May 8, facing heavy and fierce fighter opposition, he again displayed extraordinary skill as an airman and the aggressive spirit of a fighter in repeated and effectively executed counterattacks against a superior number of enemy planes in which three enemy aircraft were destroyed. Though seriously wounded in this engagement, Lt(jg) Hall, maintaining the fearless and indomitable tactics pursued throughout these actions, succeeded in landing his plane safely aboard.'

Lt John James Powers

Born: July 13, 1912, New York City

Entered Service at: New York

Other Navy Award: Air Medal with 1 gold star

Place and Date: Coral Sea area, May 4-8, 1942

Citation: 'For distinguished and conspicuous gallantry and intrepidity at the risk of his life above and beyond the call of duty, while pilot of an airplane of Bombing Squadron 5, Lt Powers participated, with his squadron, in five engagements with Japanese forces in the Coral Sea area and adjacent waters during the period 4 to 8 May 1942. Three attacks were made on enemy objectives at or near Tulagi on May 4. In these attacks he scored a direct hit which instantly demolished a large enemy gunboat and is credited with two close misses . . .

'On May 7, an attack was launched against an enemy airplane carrier and other units of the enemy's invasion force. He fearlessly led his attack section of three Douglas Dauntless dive bombers, to attack the carrier. On this occasion he dived in the face of heavy anti-aircraft fire, to an altitude well below the safety altitude, at the risk of his life and almost certain damage to his own plane, in order that he might positively obtain a hit in a vital part of the ship . . . This bomb hit was noted by many pilots and observers to cause a tremendous explosion engulfing the ship in a mass of flame, smoke and debris. The ship sank soon after.

'That evening, in his capacity as squadron gunnery officer, Lt Powers gave a lecture on point of aim and diving technique. During this discourse he advocated low release point in order to insure greater accuracy; yet he stressed the danger not only from enemy fire and the resultant low pull-out, but from own bomb blast and fragments. Thus, his low dive bombing attacks were deliberate and premeditated, since he well knew and realised the dangers of such tactics, but went far beyond the call of duty in order to further the cause which he knew to be right.

'The next morning, May 8, as the pilots of the attack group left the ready room to man planes, his indomitable spirit and leadership were well

The formidable team of Lt(jg) John Leppla and Radioman John Liska were standouts at Coral Sea. The VS-2 crew participated in the *Shoho* attack on 7 May and survived the anti-torpedo aircraft patrol the next day. Between them they were credited with seven enemy aircraft – Liska added another flying with VS-10, while Leppla was killed flying an F4F in the Santa Cruz battle that October (*Naval Aviation Museum*)

expressed in his own words, "Remember the folks back home are counting on us. I am going to get a hit if I have to lay it on their flight deck." He led his section of dive-bombers down to the target from an altitude of 18,000 ft, through a wall of bursting anti-aircraft shells and into the face of enemy fighter planes. Again, completely disregarding the safety altitude and without fear or concern for his safety, Lt Powers courageously pressed home his attack, almost to the very deck of an enemy carrier, and did not release his bomb until he was sure of a direct hit. He was last seen attempting recovery from his dive at the extremely low altitude of 200 ft, and amid a terrific barrage of shell and bomb fragments, smoke, flame and debris from the stricken vessel.'

MIDWAY

After the Coral Sea battle, Lt Wallace Short's VB-5 was retained in *Yorktown* while the rest of the air group rotated ashore. In describing the brief, hectic period at 'Pearl', Short recalled;

'We kept the remaining planes we had after Coral Sea, about 9 or 10, and drew about 10 or 12 replacements which had to be equipped with self-sealing tanks, armour plate and twin .30-cal flexible guns. The old planes got new flexible guns, too.

'Upon our sortie from Pearl, we flew our squadrons aboard and that's where most of the new pilots qualified for carrier landings.'

SBD Squadrons (Outside ConUS) – 4 June 1942

VB-3	18 SBD-3	USS *Yorktown* (CV 5)
VS-3	27 SBD-3	USS *Saratoga* (CV 5)
VB-5	19 SBD-3	USS *Yorktown* (VB 5 as VS 5)
VS-5	19 SBD-3	Hawaii
VB-6	19 SBD-3	USS *Enterprise* (CV 6)
VS-6	19 SBD-3	USS *Enterprise* (CV 6)
VB-8	19 SBD-3	USS *Hornet* (CV 8)
VS-8	19 SBD-3	USS *Hornet* (CV 8)
VMSB-231	6 SBD-1	Hawaii
VMSB-232	?	Hawaii
VMSB-233	?	Hawaii
VMSB-234	5 SBD-1	Hawaii
VMSB-241	19 SBD-2	Midway

Total - 189+

Midway's garrison scout-bombing squadron was Maj Lofton R Henderson's VMSB-241. Originally equipped with Vought SB2U-3s, the

'Baker 15' of Bombing Six taxies forward on *Yorktown* after recovery from the spectacular morning strike of 4 June at the Battle of Midway. Ens George H Goldsmith and his gunner, Radioman James W Patterson, lacked fuel to continue to *Enterprise* and barely got aboard her sister-ship. Their SBD-3 (BuNo 4542) sustained substantial battle damage during VB-6's successful attack against IJNS *Kaga*

Vindicators were augmented by 16 SBD-2s on 26 May – barely a week before the battle. With too little time and fuel for proper training, 'Joe' Henderson decided to use glide bombing tactics rather than the steeper, more difficult, 70-degree dive for which the Douglas dive-bomber was intended.

Shortly before 0600 on 4 June, Midway radar reported 'Many planes, 89 miles, bearing 320.' VMSB-241 hastily took off in two groups, Henderson's SBDs and Maj Benjamin Norris' SB2Us.

Maj Henderson led his 16 SBD-2s against heavy opposition from Zeros and shipboard anti-aircraft guns. In a running fight, casualties were inflicted on both sides as SBD gunners claimed four Zeros shot down.

Approaching the flagship *Akagi*, the Marines could see more Japanese fighters taking off. In the words of the second division leader, Capt Elmer Glidden;

'The first (enemy fighter) attacks were directed at the squadron leader in an attempt to put him out of action. After about two passes, one of the enemy put several shots through the plane of Maj Henderson, and his plane started to burn. From the actions of the leader it was apparent that he was hit and out of action. I was leader of the second box immediately behind the major. As soon as it was apparent that the major was out of action I took over the lead and continued the attack. Fighter attacks were heavy so I led the squadron down through a protecting layer of clouds and gave the signal to attack. On emerging from the cloud bank the enemy carrier was directly below the squadron, and all planes made their runs. The diving interval was about five seconds.

'Immediately after coming out from the protection of the clouds the squadron was attacked again by fighter planes and heavy AA. After making my run I kept heading on for the water, and I headed on an approximate heading home.'

Glidden's surviving pilots claimed two hits and a near miss with their 500-lb bombs, but the cost was high – upon landing at Midway, VMSB-241 had only six operational Dauntlesses and five Vindicators. The SBD-2 flown by 1st Lt Daniel Iverson Jr (BuNo 2106) returned with 259 bullet holes by actual count, and although the pilot's throat microphone was shot off his, the fortunate young man survived to fight again.

ENTERPRISE AND *YORKTOWN* WIN THE BATTLE

The carrier-based SBD squadrons were evenly matched in equipment, each with 35 to 37 aircraft, but there was considerable difference among the air groups in respect to combat experience. *Enterprise* and *Yorktown* were both battle-tested ships, and the 'Big E' possessed a high percentage of veteran aircrew. The 'Yorktowners' retained Lt Short's VB-5 as scouts, and although the fighting, bombing and torpedo squadrons were from *Saratoga*, they were skilled in carrier operations. However, *Hornet's* units were new to the fleet, and even newer to Pacific operations. Their only 'combat' to date had been the Doolittle raid in April.

On the morning of 4 June, following Midway-based PBY reports during the night, *Yorktown* (acting independently of *Enterprise* and *Hornet*) launched a ten-aircraft search composed of VB-5 and -3 aircraft. From their position northeast of Midway, they scouted to 100 miles, found nothing and returned. There was barely time to rearm the Bombing Three aircraft, as Task Force (TF) 16 and 17 were both preparing to attack Vice Adm Nagumo. His four carriers had already wrecked Midway with 107-aircraft raid.

Rear Adm Raymond Spruance's TF-16 was first off the mark. Relying on patrol aircraft reports, he calculated that the enemy carriers would appear within range to the southwest. Therefore, *Enterprise* put up a deckload strike – 33 SBDs and 14 TBDs, escorted by 10 Wildcats. Simultaneously *Hornet* prepared 34 SBDs, 15 TBDs and 10 F4Fs. Distance to the target was estimated at approximately 150 miles.

Yorktown, having to recover her morning scouts, was delayed somewhat, and her squadrons had farther to fly – about 175 miles, which was 'stretching it' for Fighting Three's six escorting F4Fs. But everyone involved recognised that the Douglas TBD-1 Devastators would need fighter escort against an alerted enemy force.

At this point things began to unravel for the Americans. Land-based attacks on the Japanese force had impeded its forward advance, owing to the need to manoeuvre while dodging bombs and torpedoes from B-17s, B-26s, TBFs and the Marine scout-bombers. No damage was inflicted by Midway squadrons, but Nagumo's formation became somewhat dispersed, and much of the combat air patrol was drawn to low altitude.

Meanwhile, both TF-16 air groups were diluted by launch delays and airborne errors. Looking down through patchy clouds, *Enterprise's* F4Fs unknowingly followed *Hornet's* Devastators, leaving Torpedo 6 unescorted. Simultaneously, the *Hornet* air group commander with the SBDs and his fighter skipper gradually diverged from the purposeful Lt Cdr J C Waldron of VT-8. The net result – other than Torpedo Eight, Hornet Air Group played no significant part in the battle.

Yorktown's experienced air staff under Rear Adm F J Fletcher managed things better. They decided on a 'running rendezvous', rather than circling the task force while the entire strike group was launched. Consequently, Bombing Three, Torpedo Three and Fighting Three arrived intact near the enemy screen, having flown a more direct route to the target. Lt Cdrs M F Leslie, L E Massey and J S Thach conducted the only co-ordinated American attack of the day. Fortuitously combined with the *Enterprise* squadrons, it achieved spectacular results.

THE LONG HUNT

Leading 32 SBDs of VB- and VS-6 was Lt Cdr C W McClusky, until very recently the skipper of VF-6. Search conditions were excellent, with a clear sky above a patchy layer of low-lying clouds.

McClusky had departed TF-16 at about 0755, steering a southwesterly

Lt Richard H Best commanded Bombing Six during most of *Enterprise's* combat in the first six months of the Pacific War. On 4 June he led attacks that contributed to the sinking of *Akagi* and *Hiryu*, but was immediately grounded with tuberculosis caused by a freak accident with his aircraft's oxygen system. Medically retired as a lieutenant commander, he is acknowledged as having been one of the finest dive-bomber pilots to serve with the Pacific fleet (*Naval Aviation Museum*)

CHAPTER THREE

Commanding VB-3 at Midway was Lt Cdr Maxwell F Leslie, who led *Yorktown's* SBDs in the morning strike against the Japanese carriers on 4 June. Leslie and three other pilots lost their bombs en route to the target owing to faulty electrical arming systems, but they continued with the mission regardless. The *Yorktown* attack group approached *Kido Butai* from the southeast, while *Enterprise* squadrons struck from the southwest. Although Torpedo Three was nearly destroyed, VB-3 attacked unhindered and sank IJNS *Soryu*. Leslie subsequently became Enterprise air group commander for the Guadalcanal campaign

This frame taken from rare Midway film footage recorded by a newsreel cameraman shows VS-8 aircraft over the doomed Japanese battlecruiser *Mikuma* during the afternoon of 6 June. A submarine alarm caused a collision with her sister *Mogami* early on the morning of the 5th, leaving both ships vulnerable. Combined strikes by Midway aircraft in concert with *Enterprise* and *Hornet* SBDs sank *Mikuma*, which absorbed enormous bomb damage

Nagumo after attacking a US submarine. Within minutes Wade McClusky had his binoculars on the circular disposition of four Japanese carriers.

Approaching *Kido Butai*, the Americans' luck continued to wane. Another SBD, flown by Ens T F Schneider, suffered engine failure and dropped away, leaving McClusky with 31 aircraft. Meanwhile Lt R H Best, leading VB-6, inhaled caustic soda fumes from a faulty oxygen bottle – the long-term effects would be catastrophic to his flying career.

As if that were not enough, Lt Cdr Leslie's VB-3 formation, though intact, had lost nearly one quarter of its striking power. Once clear of TF-17, his pilots threw the electrical arming switches in their cockpits, but Leslie and three other pilots had felt their bombs abruptly drop toward the sea.

More by luck than design, the TF-16 and -17 strike groups approached *Kido Butai* from opposite quarters almost simultaneously. Torpedo Eight and Six attacked first, drawing the A6M2 defenders nearly to wavetop height while flak guns were depressed. Shortly thereafter, VT-3 arrived and was similarly shot to pieces with no torpedo hits on any enemy ships.

By now the Japanese had reason to feel confident – they had shot down 15 Midway fighters, 18 land-based attack aircraft and 35 carrier torpedo aircraft. Despite the intensive combat, no imperial carrier had even been damaged.

Then Nagumo's lookouts and gun captains felt their hearts rise in their throats – overhead, three squadrons of Dauntless dive-bombers were plunging down on three carriers, completely unopposed. Caught with strike groups fuelled and armed for an attack on the US task forces, the Japanese were appallingly vulnerable.

It was over in less than six minutes. McClusky led the *Enterprise* SBDs against the flagship *Akagi* and *Kaga*, whilst Leslie, without a bomb, took VB-3 down on *Soryu*. A mix-up in attack doctrine among the 'Big E's' Dauntlesses resulted in 28 hammering *Kaga*, while only Lt Best's three-SBD section went after *Akagi*. It didn't matter – both ships were gutted by bomb hits and uncontrollable fires. So was *Soryu*, which was so embroiled in smoke and flame that the last few VB-3 pilots diverted in their dives to battleships or cruisers.

Pulling off-target, the *Enterprise* men had a low-level gunfight on their hands. McClusky was wounded in one shoulder and his new gunner, Radioman WG Chochalousek, added to the damage by trying to fire his twin-.30-cal mount either side of the vertical stabiliser – unsuccessfully!

Some of the Zeros performed exceptional stunts. Upon overshooting the slow weaving SBDs, A6Ms only 500 ft above the wavetops would loop back for another pass. In all, 16 of McClusky's 32 SBDs that reached *Kido Butai* succumbed to fighters or empty tanks, and some of the returnees would not fly again soon. Wade McClusky barely got aboard the 'Big E' with five gallons remaining and a bullet in his left shoulder.

Bombing Three got off much easier. Upon return to TF-17, Leslie and his wingman, Lt(jg) Paul Holmberg, circled a downed VT-3 Devastator long enough to attract a destroyer, but then lacked enough gasoline to return to *Yorktown*. They ditched alongside the cruiser *Astoria* and were immediately rescued.

The other dozen Bombing Three aircraft safely trapped aboard *Enterprise*, where they were sorely needed. During their return flight, IJNS *Hiryu* launched an effective bombing attack which, despite losing 13 of 18 Aichi D3As, left 'Old Yorky' dead in the water. It was still a battle – two depleted air groups against *Hiryu*. *Hornet's* SBDs found nothing and straggled into Midway or back to the ship, having lost three Dauntlesses and all ten Wildcats to fuel exhaustion.

Aboard *Enterprise*, surviving VB- and VS-6 crews patched together an impromptu organisation with the VB-3 overflow. With McClusky in the sick bay, seniority fell to Lt Earl Gallaher, skipper of Scouting Six, who made preparations for a strike as soon as *Hiryu* was located. That information shortly arrived from a VB-5 team led by Lt Samuel Adams, who found her due west of TF-16. However, *Hiryu's* efficient air department had launched a hasty mission of Nakajima B5Ns, which again found *Yorktown* and torpedoed her. This time she was truly out of the battle.

Twenty-four SBDs, minus fighter escort, departed *Enterprise* at 1530, and 16 *Hornet* aircraft followed a half-hour later. Diving from 19,000 ft, Gallaher took his own crews against the carrier, directing Lt D W Shumway's VB-3 to the most prominent escort. Zeros intercepted, downing a VB-6 SBD, but by then the Dauntlesses were slanting down through the reddening sky.

Gallaher's pilots secured at least one hit, but Shumway, perceiving a need for reinforcements, abruptly switched to the carrier. Between them, VB-3 and VB-6 got three or four more hits and *Hiryu* erupted in volcanic flames fed by fuel and ordnance. Two VB-3 aircraft later succumbed to Zeros during the retirement.

Hornet's tardy strike arrived as *Enterprise's* aircraft withdrew, missed the heavy cruiser *Tone*, then followed Gallaher's units back to the task force.

Not everyone knew it yet, but the Battle of Midway had been won.

THREE DAYS TO VICTORY

Throughout Friday the 5th, the US task force had two main concerns: relocating the Japanese and saving *Yorktown*. When a sighting was made (what subsequently turned out to be a false alarm about an enemy carrier), a late afternoon launch proceeded with 64 SBDs from *Enterprise* and *Hornet*. Most of *Hornet's* aircraft found nothing, but 43 SBDs attacked the lone destroyer *Tanikaze*, which led a charmed life – Lt Adams, who had found *Hiryu* the day before, was killed in the action, along with his gunner, Radioman J J Karrol. A night recovery was safely effected aboard both US carriers.

At 0700 the next morning, 6 June, VMSB-241 scrambled six Dauntlesses and six Vindicators in response to a report of Japanese warships limping westward about 170 miles from Midway. The Marines found the cruisers *Mogami* and *Mikuma* trailing oil after a nocturnal collision, and Capt Tyler quickly led his SBDs down from 10,000 ft while the half-dozen SB2Us began a shallow approach from 4000 ft. Each of the Dauntless pilots claimed a near miss on *Mogami*, while the SB2U leader, Capt Richard E Fleming, crashed into *Mikuma*. Because his action was deemed intentional, he was awarded a posthumous Medal of Honor.

Navy SBDs finished off the battered cruiser later that day, and although *Yorktown* and the destroyer *Hammann* had been sunk, 6 June wrote a conclusive finish to the climactic Battle of Midway.

Saratoga loads aircraft at Pearl Harbor on 6 June 1942, hastily preparing to reinforce the Midway task force. Many of these SBDs were delivered to *Enterprise* and *Hornet* on the 11th, replacing heavy combat and operational losses. The Dauntless being craned aboard has unusual markings, including a rare version of the LSO stripe, which was normally placed higher on the vertical stabiliser

GUADALCANAL AND THE SOLOMONS

Guadalcanal, in the Solomon Islands, became the focus of Allied and Japanese land, naval and air activity beginning in August 1942. The ensuing six-month campaign involved jungle warfare, surface engagements and naval air activity on almost a daily basis. Guadalcanal was the crucible of combined arms operations for the Allies and Japan, and in the end the Americans did it better than the Japanese.

However, in the early engagements the Japanese decidedly held the edge. When the Marines went ashore on 7 August, Vice Adm Fletcher's three carriers immediately established air supremacy as *Enterprise*, *Wasp* and *Saratoga* overwhelmed the small Japanese floatplane unit at Tulagi. But that day Rabaul-based bombers and fighters struck back hard. Seventeen Zeroes of the Tainan Wing shot down nine of eighteen Wildcats engaged, losing two A6Ms. Additionally, a *Wasp* SBD was lost with the gunner killed. VS-71 aviator, Lt Dudley Adams, surprised a flight led by Petty Officer 1st Class Saburo Sakai, but was shot down by the Japanese

By the start of the Guadalcanal campaign in August 1942, Scouting Five was a combat-seasoned unit. Lt Cdr Turner Caldwell's squadron had flown from *Yorktown* through Coral Sea, then embarked in *Enterprise* for Operation *Watchtower*, and provided much of the fabled Flight 300 that operated ashore with the Marines. Seated in front are Caldwell and his gunner, Chief Radioman W E Glidewell (*Naval Aviation Museum*)

SCOUTING SQUADRON JULY 5 1942

Flight Chief Petty Officer Saburo Sakai was among the Imperial Navy's leading fighter pilots by the summer of 1942. A combat veteran dating from China in 1938, Sakai had destroyed or damaged some 50 Allied aircraft by the time he engaged F4Fs and SBDs over Guadalcanal on 7 August 1942. Early in the mission he shot down a VF-5 Wildcat and a VS-71 SBD, but then, as he approached a formation of *Enterprise* Dauntlesses, he was spotted and taken under fire by multiple gunners. Grievously wounded, he managed to fly 550 miles to Rabaul, New Britain, and returned to combat two years later (*Henry Sakaida*)

ace. Sakai was a highly experienced fighter pilot, with 50 or more Chinese, American and other Allied aircraft destroyed or damaged since 1938 (see *Osprey Aircraft of the Aces 22 - Imperial Japanese Navy Aces 1937-45* by Henry Sakaida for further details).

Sakai then spotted a formation of what he assumed were F4Fs and approached from six o'clock low. However, his intended victims were alert and saw him coming. They were eight *Enterprise* SBDs of VB-6 and VS-5, led by Lt Carl Horenburger, circling Tulagi awaiting orders to attack a target.

Sakai and his wingman, Petty Officer 2nd Class Enji Kakimoto, were barely within range when the rear gunners opened fire. Two SBDs were damaged, one losing its place in the formation, but Sakai's cockpit absorbed multiple .30-cal hits. Severely wounded, he dropped from nearly 8000 ft to almost sea level, before pulling out. His 550-mile return flight to Rabaul became an epic of aviation survival.

MANGRUM AT GUADALCANAL

Richard C Mangrum enlisted in the USMC directly from college in 1928, and by late 1941 was an experienced aviator with some 3000 flight hours. He was with VMSB-232 throughout 1941, based at Ewa, Hawaii, between 'Pearl' and Barbers Point. Equipped with SBD-1s, the squadron lost nearly all its aircraft in the Sunday morning attack of 7 December.

Mangrum assumed command of the 'Red Devils' in January 1942, and fought a continuing battle to retain enough aircrew, mechanics and aircraft to meet any assignment. Finally, in July -232 received the last dozen SBD-3s from the fleet pool and prepared to embark in the escort carrier *Long Island*. On 20 August Mangrum's dozen Dauntlesses and VMF-223's F4F-4s catapulted from the 'baby flattop' to become the first contingent of the 'Cactus Air Force';

'We had no information whatever about Guadalcanal. To be sure, the general concept of Marine Corps operations and training and planning envisions rough field conditions – just how rough sometimes is a bit shocking even to Marines!

'There were no vehicles for fuelling and arming, thus these functions were tedious and time consuming. Ordnance and fuel drums had to be manhandled, and there wasn't any manpower. Fuel was hand-pumped from drums, and the pumps quickly wore out. Fatigue of personnel, plus lack of adequate food or rest, made for a descending spiral which accounted, with losses incident to operations, for the relatively short sojourn of the first units in the Battle for Guadalcanal.

'The runway at Henderson Field, such as it was, was rough, and loose gravel abounded. The undersides of our aircraft were soon in a shocking condition: landing flaps, for example, were in shreds. Parking areas were dirt – either mud or dust, or both at once. Maintenance for anything but the prime essentials was impossible. But the Dauntless never let us down. Fortunately, the handful of squadron mechanics who were brought up from Efate by destroyer, and who had to carry the whole load for the first two weeks, were experienced old timers, and they were magnificent. And they had to take on Lt Turner Caldwell's Flight 300 from *Enterprise* as well – a blessed reinforcement for our bob-tailed squadron, but they joined us without even so much as a toothbrush.'

Leading *Enterprise* Flight 319 on 7 August was Lt Carl Horenberger of VB-6, whose eight SBDs (including two of VS-5) were attacked by Sakai and Petty Officer Enji Kakimoto. Two Dauntlesses were damaged by Japanese gunfire, but both continued their mission. The Zero pilots claimed two kills, while the 'Big E' aircrews thought they had destroyed Sakai's A6M2, but in fact no aircraft were lost from this brief encounter (*Henry Sakaida*)

No glamour for the 'Cactus Air Force'. This late 1942 photo aptly displays the environment of Henderson Field, Guadalcanal – muddy parking area, and canvas shelters on the higher ground nearest the camera. All of the SBDs in the photo apparently belong to the same unit, as they bear a uniform style and placement of white identification numbers immediately aft of the fuselage star

Aside from the Japanese, the Marine aviators found the Solomons' weather a factor in operations. Mangrum's unit found 'typical tropical stuff – high-altitude build-ups mostly in the afternoon and early part of the night, and thunder showers, usually widely scattered, sometimes thicker particularly when close to the island. Usually flights could detour around the build-ups. I can't remember anybody being stuck, out of fuel, waiting for a dense shower to clear the airfield. Once only during our stay we had to abort a mission due to a severe line squall which prevented us getting out to the north. I lost two planes, however, and their crews, to weather. They tried to barge through a build-up and apparently it had a hard core.'

On 25 August – the sixth day ashore – VMSB-232 launched its first major attack on Japanese shipping. Mangrum led the mission, and although his bomb failed to release, he remained in the area and returned to attack again, succeeding in dropping his bomb. This action subsequently earned him a Medal of Honor recommendation. He recalled;

'Sketchy intelligence reports indicated the presence of large Japanese task forces intending a major attack to recapture Guadalcanal, and we were out looking for them. The beach-head was shelled by a cruiser and destroyer force during the night, and we took off after them, but I doubt that we accomplished much more than astonish the hell out of them. What moon there was was low, and visibility was practically nil, although we did bomb and strafe them in the Florida Strait.

This SBD-3, fully armed with a 500-pounder on the centreline and two 100-pounders beneath the wings, receives last-minute attention from shirtless marines. The aircraft is obviously well used, with faded paint and caked-on oil streaks. The side number 41 has been crudely applied in white paint aft of the fuselage star. The assigned unit is impossible to determine, partly because SBD crews often flew other squadrons' aircraft, depending upon availability

'This is to say that for about two days there was practically no maintenance done – we just flew them as they were. The SBD bomb release was mechanical: yank a lever connected by wire to the release. So dirt in the works may have contributed. Maybe I simply didn't yank hard enough. I simply don't know why the bomb hung up, as it used to happen occasionally. At any rate, it released all right when I went back with it.'

Fortunately, aerial opposition was infrequent for Dauntless crews at 'Cactus'. Throughout the six-month Guadalcanal campaign, Marine SBD squadrons claimed some 26 aerial victories, including two by VMSB-232. Summarised Mangrum;

'There were enough clouds to lurk behind in those pre-radar days. Rear guns wouldn't have helped us much, and we knew it, so evasion was the best answer, including getting down close to the surface. We thought it would be nice to have fighter escort when we went somewhere. But the essential task of our fighters was to protect the beach-head against air attack, and they were superb in the job. There were none available to provide cover for SBDs. Conversely, the primary task of Japanese fighters was to protect their bombers, and Guadalcanal was at about their maximum radius of action. Thus, they had no time to go after us, and we could usually keep out of their way, or seek some friendly clouds if some stray hostile showed up.

'The fact is that the squadron was pretty well used up a month before it was evacuated. New units began feeding into Guadalcanal by September and began to take over the principal air operations. The First Marine Air Wing was then in operation, and remnants of units operated directly under Brig Gen Roy Geiger. Marine Air Group 23, of which VMSB-232 was a part, was by mid-September pretty much a collection of remnants. I had lost most of my pilots – some through combat, some from night shelling, some from accident. Two or three of us did some flying after mid-September, but in the main the fresh units carried the load. I did no flying in October, I believe. The squadron officially departed Guadalcanal on 13 October by ship. I left on 14 October by air in order to collect some wounded men in the Efate hospital, thence to Noumea to rejoin the rest of the outfit.'

The logbook of Mangrum's flight officer, Capt Bruce Prosser, demonstrates the intensity of 'Cactus' operations. In 29 days ashore, between 20 August and 17 September, he flew 28 missions, including ten strikes (three ant-shipping), eight searches ('To see if we or the Japanese were getting supplied that day'), seven reconnaissance flights in support of the infantry and anti-submarine patrols.

EASTERN SOLOMONS

The first carrier battle of the campaign occurred on 24 August, only four days after VMSB-232 and VMF-223 landed at Henderson Field. On the

Four stalwarts of the 'Cactus Air Force'. From left to right, Lt Col Richard C Mangrum, Maj Robert W Vaupell, Maj John L Smith and Capt Joseph J Foss. Smith and Foss received Medals of Honor for their records as fighter pilots, while Mangrum and Vaupell were leading SBD pilots. Vaupell was later killed commanding VMSB-233 in 1945. Mangrum led VMSB-232, the first bombing squadron ashore at Guadalcanal. Operating from Henderson Field between late August and late October 1942, the squadron maintained offensive sorties despite a chronic shortage of spare parts, tools and mechanics. Concluded Mangrum, 'The Dauntless kept us in business – we just flew 'em as they were' (*Peter B Mersky via Dennis Byrd*)

23rd, PBY Catalinas reported Japanese naval units and transports advancing southward from the Rabaul area.

The US task force was down to two flight decks, as Vice Adm Fletcher had detached *Wasp* for refuelling. Thus, on the day of battle, *Saratoga* was designated the attack carrier while *Enterprise* conducted reconnaissance. That afternoon six SBD-3s of Bombing Six and seven of Scouting Five launched at 1320, searching to 250 miles. All three VB-6 search teams contacted the enemy.

The first search team, scouting the 340-350-degree sector, was Lt Ray Davis and his wingman, Ens R C Shaw. They reported;

'At 1500 ft located enemy force at Lat 5-45 South, Longitude 162-10 East, speed 28 knots, course 120 True, and started to attack one of the two leading CLs when they sighted a large CV of about 20,000 tons behind the CLs. The two planes then circled and climbed to attack the CV. Lt Davis, followed by Ens Shaw, dove at the CV from upwind, down-sun at 1545 from 14,000 ft, then released two 500-lb bombs with

USS *Saratoga* (CV 3) was active with the Pacific Fleet from 1941 to 1945, but logged much of her combat off Guadalcanal during 1942. Her air group supported the initial landings on 7 August, and fought the Eastern Solomons battle barely two weeks later. She was torpedoed for the second time late that month and withdrew for repairs. In this 1943 photo, her SBDs and TBFs are being ranged forward on the flight deck

1/100 second delayed-action fuse at 2000 ft and made low pull-outs, high-speed withdrawals out over the general direction of the easternmost leading CL.

'Lt Davis' bomb hit not more than five feet off the starboard side aft of amidships of the CV. Ens Shaw's bomb hit not more than 20 ft off the starboard quarter of the CV, close to Lt Davis' bomb. Two water splashes were seen; only a column of smoke was observed. The CV was turning to starboard when Lt Davis began his dive, and during his dive from 7000 ft to 2000 ft the CV made a 60-degree turn. Jones, AOM2c, rearseat gunner, observed eight planes amidships and twelve spotted aft on the flight deck of the CV attacked. Heavy AA fire from the CV was seen, the small stuff being accurate and the heavy stuff inaccurate. The AA fire of the easternmost CL, when the planes were retiring over that ship, was fairly accurate. There were seven or eight planes in the air over the CV, and one, a Zero, began a run on the retiring planes, but AA fire from the forward CL brought the enemy plane down.

'The enemy force consisted of two large CV, four CA, six CL and eight DD (actually *Shokaku* and *Zuikaku* with five destroyers.) Lt Davis reported that he transmitted to the *Enterprise* his location of the enemy force before they made their attack on the carrier. After their attack, Lt Davis transmitted a report of the two bombs he and Ens Shaw dropped near the CV.'

In the adjacent, northernmost sector, Lt J T Lowe Jr and Ens R D Gibson found a large surface force, reported as three cruisers, three to five destroyers and other ships (actually five cruisers, a light cruiser and six destroyers, plus a seaplane carrier.) The crews reported;

'The enemy force was making about 20 knots on a course of 180 True. B-13 (Lowe) and B-5 (Gibson) were on a course 000; they circled to the east, climbed to 11,000 ft and approached the largest CA – possibly the *Atago* – down-sun. At 1510, both planes dove, released two 500-lb bombs with 1/100 seconds delayed action fuse at 2500 ft, then glided to 20 ft altitude and retired to the south. Lt Lowe's bomb hit about 20 yards off the CA's starboard quarter. Ens Gibson's bomb hit within 25 ft off the CA's port bow; the spray from the bomb hit came up over the bow. The CA kept her beam to the planes, and while the planes were diving, the CA made an abrupt turn to starboard, skidding around, and reversed course. The AA fire was of both heavy and light stuff. It was not effective; most of it was short.'

Both bombs near-missed the 10,000-ton cruiser *Maya*. Gibson ran out of fuel on the return leg and ditched near destroyer *Farragut*. Two VB-6 SBDs intercepted Japanese aircraft retiring from their attack on *Enterprise*, whilst the other pair found no enemy forces.

'CSAG' was the unofficial title of Cdr Harry Don Felt, Commander Saratoga Air Group during the Guadalcanal campaign. Here, he is joined by Chief Radioman Cletus A Snyder aboard 'Queen Bee' (SBD-3 BuNo 03213) shortly after the Eastern Solomons campaign. Whilst flying this aircraft, Felt and Snyder led 'Sara's' squadrons in the sinking of IJNS *Ryujo* on 24 August. Felt was among the earliest SBD pilots, having led VB-2 when *Lexington* received her initial 'dash twos' in late 1940

RYUJO SUNK

At 1430 *Saratoga's* air group commander, Harry D Felt, led 30 SBDs and eight TBFs in pursuit of a reported enemy carrier. Of 13 Bombing Three pilots on the mission, ten were veterans of Midway, led by the CO, Lt Cdr D W Shumway, and the second division under Lt H S Bottomley Jr. The balance of the strike group involved Scouting Three SBDs and seven Torpedo Eight TBFs, one of which aborted.

Sighting the *Ryujo* group at 1610, Felt deployed 21 SBDs and five TBFs against the CVL. The second division of VB-3 (seven SBDs) and two Avengers was assigned the largest escort – the cruiser *Tone*. Two destroyers also accompanied the group, while seven airborne Zeros were unable to intervene.

Despite the large number of bombers attacking the carrier, only near misses were observed. Therefore, Cdr Felt redirected the other aircraft, as noted in the action report;

'Just as the second division of VB-3 commenced its attack on the cruiser, it was ordered to shift its objective to the carrier. This squadron made diving attacks from 15,000 ft in various directions on the carrier objective. Average release altitudes were 2000 ft with retirements close to the water at high speeds. Moderate A fire was encountered during the action.

'About four Nakajima 97s were observed being launched just prior to the attack and made ineffective passes during dive-bombing recoveries. One of this type was shot down by Godfrey, J V, ARM3/c, gunner of B-35, and confirmed by his pilot, Ens A W Hanson. No air opposition was encountered at altitude. The enemy manoeuvred radically at high speed during the attack, generally in tight clockwise circles.

'Thirteen 1000-lb demolition bombs (seven with Mk 19 and 23 contact fuses and six with Mk 21 and 23 contact fuses) were dropped, and 400 rounds of .30-cal machine gun ammunition was expended. Three direct bomb hits and several very close misses were observed. It is estimated that two additional direct hits were made. A torpedo hit was observed on the starboard side forward on the carrier, and it is believed that one additional hit was also scored on the carrier. The carrier flight deck from amidships aft was smoking fiercely and flames were seen to be shooting out from the hangar deck. Planes rendezvoused in small groups and proceeded to their base.'

The attackers' claims were unusually accurate – probably three bombs struck the CVL, as did one torpedo. *Tone* was unscratched.

Returning home, a group of ten SBDs encountered four Aichi D3As after attacking *Enterprise*. Between them, VS-3 and VB-3 claimed four shootdowns, and while no 'Vals' were actually lost, it ended a highly satisfactory mission without friendly casualties.

An SBD-3 on an evening flight over the Pacific Ocean. This photo was taken from the section leader's aircraft, probably whilst on a scouting or training mission owing to the lack of ordnance. Doctrine called for two-aircraft teams to be assigned to each search sector in order to provide mutual support and navigation

Finally, two VB-3 Dauntlesses and five Avengers scrambled off *Saratoga* at 1700, hunting a large surface force. At 1810 a Japanese unit was seen through low clouds, estimated at one battleship, five cruisers and six destroyers. In truth they were *Mutsu* (correctly identified), and the 11,000-ton seaplane carrier *Chitose*, plus four destroyers.

Led by Lt(jg) Robert M Elder, another Midway veteran, the small strike group delivered a co-ordinated attack;

'Upon passing into a clear area the entire disposition was revealed. At 1820 approach was made from the west at 12,500 ft. There was no aircraft opposition, but AA fire was extremely heavy. The dive-bombing attack was made from the west, release altitude was 2000 ft, and retirement effected to the eastward, manoeuvring radically at low altitude and high speed. Two 1000-lb demolition bombs (Mk 21 and 23 contact fuses) were dropped. One direct hit was observed on the battleship, aft of the stack on the port side. One possible hit was made on the starboard side amidships. Intense smoke was seen for a short period abaft the stack. Both planes returned to the *Saratoga* and were landed aboard during darkness.'

Actually, Elder and Ens R T Gordon near-missed *Chitose*, well astern of the battleship group. The bombs opened her hull and started a fire that destroyed aircraft on deck. The ship was out of commission for months.

GIBSON'S VIEW

Ens Robert D Gibson was one of the most experienced combat SBD pilots in the Navy. Flying from *Enterprise* with VB-6, he participated in the Eastern Solomons battle and then went ashore with Flight 300 on Guadalcanal. Subsequently joining VB-10, Gibson was involved at Santa Cruz as well. His recommendations were recorded in a VB-6 action report;

'When the enemy is known, or believed to be in an area, a single plane might be sent out on each 10-degree sector. At the same time, an attack group might be launched and this group proceed along a line bearing on the enemy's position as designated by the previous contact. The attack group would therefore most likely follow along the median of the search sector, since the sector would be fanned out to cover the area most likely to hold the enemy. Therefore, when any of the scouts made contact with the enemy force, that plane could immediately radio the attack group which would be following rather closely. In this way we can avoid the enemy's being amply forewarned by their discovery of our scouts over their position, and we can eliminate the delay in transmitting the enemy's position back to the carrier. This delay now enables the enemy force to launch planes and attack our carrier while we are attacking theirs, or it enables the enemy to change their course and prevent later contacts. Under the above plan, once our scouts contact the enemy, we will have an attack group near the scene for a quick and, perhaps, surprise attack.

'While retiring from a dive-bombing attack, if the plane will fly into the area of shrapnel of the AA shells previously fired – provided, of course, that he does not fly into the shrapnel still falling in that area – he will avoid the enemy's corrected fire. As the enemy notes that their fire is inaccurate, they will correct and compensate in their next fire; if the pilot flies into the area of their previous firing it is believed he will most probably keep out of their subsequent fire.

Lt Robert M Elder was one of the most accomplished aviators of World War 2. He flew with VB-3 at Midway and the Eastern Solomons battles, leading a two-SBD attack on a Japanese force on 24 August. Subsequently, he became a test pilot, proving the concept of the 'Seahorse' variant of the P-51 Mustang, before flying early jets. He served as captain of USS *Coral Sea* (CVA 43) postwar, before retiring to head Northrop's flight test division. There, he was instrumental in the development of Northrop's YF-17, which led to the F/A-18 Hornet strike fighter

'Aiming in dive-bombing – the bombs will hit where the pipper is. The bomb falls so quickly that excessive allowances for wind and ship speed are likely to cause misses.'

FLIGHT 300 AND FRIENDS

As Mangrum acknowledged, a major player in the 'Cactus Air Force' was *Enterprise's* Flight 300 – a mixture of eight Scouting Five and three Bombing Six crews under VS-5's Lt Turner F Caldwell. Flown ashore on 24 August amid the confusion of the Eastern Solomons carrier battle, Flight 300 (so named for its sequence on the monthly operations plan) soon made itself felt. On the 25th Caldwell's pilots sank the transport *Kinryu Maru*, while Mangrum's Marines damaged the light carrier *Jintsu*.

Three days later Flight 300 put under destroyer *Asagiri* and damaged *Shirakumo*, while VMSB-232 also hit *Yugiri*. These losses convinced Japanese planners that daylight surface transport was fruitless as long as the Americans retained control of Henderson Field. Flight 300 remained ashore until 27 September – 35 days of almost uninterrupted combat and perennially rough conditions well beyond that expected of carrier aviators.

Four other Navy SBD squadrons operated from Henderson Field during the campaign;

VS-3

Detached from *Saratoga* after her late August torpedo damage, Lt Cdr L J Kirn's unit was sent to Espiritu Santo. However, the perennial shortage of

A Scouting Ten Dauntless is seen overhead *Enterprise* in October 1942. This particular aircraft (S-13) played an important part in the Battle of Santa Cruz, fought on the 27th. Flown by Lt S B Strong, 'Sail 13' was part of a two-aircraft search team which copied a contact report of Japanese carriers in an adjacent sector. Strong led Ens Charles Irvine to the enemy decoy force and made a successful attack upon IJNS *Zuiho*, escaping unharmed

aircraft at Guadalcanal resulted in the squadron being sent to Henderson Field from 6 September to 17 October.

VS-71

Following *Wasp's* sinking on 15 September, Lt Cdr John Eldridge took 11 crews to 'Cactus' from 28 September to 7 November. During his time at Guadalcanal, Eldridge became one of the 'Cactus Air Force's' most effective strike leaders.

VB-10

Off *Enterprise* under the control of Lt Cdr J A Thomas, 13-16 November.

VS-10

Off *Enterprise* under the control of Lt Cdr J R Lee, 13-16 November.

MORE MARINES

Five additional Marine SBD squadrons arrived at 'Cactus' during September through to December. In order of arrival they were;

VMSB-231

The second Marine scout-bomber squadron ashore, Maj Leo R Smith's 16 SBDs landed on 30 August. Three pilots were lost and one wounded before -231 was relieved on 16 October. Capt Ruben Iden relieved Maj Smith, but was lost when he ditched at sea on 20 September. Midway veteran Capt Elmer Glidden then assumed command.

VMSB-141

The largest squadron to operate from Guadalcanal during 1942, with 39 crews. The advance element arrived 23 September while the CO, Maj Gordon Bell, followed 5-6 October with the balance of the unit. During nearly two months at Henderson Field, VMSB-141 lost 14 crews, including all its senior officers during the Japanese bombardment of 14 October. Bell's successor, Lt W S Ashcraft, was killed on 8 November. The last personnel left the island on the 19th.

VMSB-132

Maj Joseph Sailer arrived at 'Cactus' with the initial cadre of his unit on 1 November. Two pilots were lost that month, and Sailer was killed in action in early December. He was succeeded by Capt L B Robertshaw.

VMSB-142

Maj Robert H Richard's ten SBDs were the last Dauntlesses thrown into the major phase of the campaign, arriving on 12 November. With no known combat losses during 1942, the squadron remained at Henderson Field into late April 1943.

VMSB-233

Arriving 12 December, Maj Clyde T Mattison's squadron was too late for the final Japanese attempt to reinforce Guadalcanal, but remained in the Pacific until March 1944. By that time the squadron had been re-equipped with Avengers and redesignated VMTB-233.

THE NAVY ASHORE

Lt Cdr Louis J Kirn's Scouting Three operated from Henderson Field from 6 September to 17 October. Kirn's subsequent report stated;

'We were faced with the problem of trying to find someplace to stay, and someone to feed us. CUB-1 had a detachment there which was supposed to have some aviation maintenance men. We found they were occupied with unloading ships most of the time, or carrying ammunition to the various dumps, and they did have some fuelling details. The Marines weren't able to take care of our maintenance problems, or feed us, but they did supply us with a couple of tents and some cots. Some of us brought cots and mosquito netting up from Espiritu Santo in anticipation of the shortage at Guadalcanal.

'Our existence there was very uncertain. The organisation on the field and the operations were very much confused because we had various squadrons there. I had my own, and the remains of two Marine squadrons, and there were also remnants of a Navy scouting and bombing squadron (Flight 300) that had come in after the *Enterprise* was damaged on 24 August. So our combat organisations were made up of anybody that was available and fit to fly, and governed mostly by the number of planes we had available.

'Our operations tent on the field was in the centre of a dust collecting area, and we were surrounded by machine gun ammunition and bombs. It didn't seem to bother us much at the time. We fell in with the atmosphere of the place, and we accepted this as normal living conditions.

'Our operations consisted of searching for the enemy, then going out and attacking. For the five weeks we were there, we conducted 20 attacks on at least 94 ships. The composite character of the flights of course precluded any one squadron taking credit for the mission. In other words, my own squadron was represented in all these attacks but did not conduct all of the exclusively. Sometimes we would form the whole attack group which may have consisted of six or seven airplanes.

'Our attacks during this period were not as effectual as we might have hoped. We were up against the problem of not having enough airplanes and pilots to carry out the destruction that we wanted to effect. We found that there were ample targets. However, they were usually the fast, highly manoeuvrable destroyers, and it was aggravating to go out and attack time after time and make good bombing runs and still see your bomb result in a near miss.

'Our tactics were to concentrate our few planes (sometimes only five or six) on one ship. We couldn't divide our attack any other way. . . We didn't know what planes we were going to have so we drew up tentative flights and appointed an experienced pilot to lead each one. Then, if a contact was sent in, we merely had time to tell the group where we would rendezvous and then give the details on the attack just prior to making it.

'The conduct of personnel there, including the few maintenance people and the gunners, was really very commendable. Despite some of the pilots getting sort of a self-pitying attitude, that was not too prevalent. But the condition did exist, and it was necessary to get rid of those one or two that we observed in that condition in order not to contaminate the rest of them. But outside of that, we found that the men never complained except what they would ordinarily complain about, regardless of where they were. But they were never reluctant to take on any assignment they were asked to do.'

RATE OF ATTRITION

Guadalcanal SBD squadrons lost at least 45 pilots and 29 gunners from August through to November. Dozens of others were evacuated with wounds or illness.

The inordinate pilot casualty rate suffered by VMSB-141 (66 per cent) demonstrates the varied risks encountered at Guadalcanal. In September 1942 the squadron left the US with 43 pilots, some of whom had only logged ten hours in dive-bombers. One aviator developed 'war neurosis' in New Caledonia – still more than 1000 miles from Guadalcanal – and another was lost on launch from escort carrier *Copahee*. Additionally, three enlisted men were killed in an R4D (C-47) crash in Samoa.

Attrition among VMSB-141 aviators covered the gamut from flying accidents to enemy action to weather – 27 pilots killed and nine evacuated in less than five weeks from 2 October to 13 November. Three-fourths of the pilots contracted malaria, and though only two were evacuated with the disease, more would have been except for lack of replacements.

Additionally, 19 gunners were killed or missing while one ground officer died in the bombardment and another broke a leg.

The constant losses and succession of commanding officers (ten in six weeks) was a drain on morale. Combined with crude living conditions, poor food and an unrelenting flight schedule (the average pilot time was about 100 hours in that period), the overall effect was debilitating. Yet the surviving aircrews pressed ahead, flying two or three hours almost every day. Noted a flight surgeon;

'The pilots were pushed beyond human endurance under the most unfavourable circumstances, confronted with the almost daily loss of their friends, yet performed a remarkable task in their share of holding Guadalcanal when the outcome was often in doubt.'

OCTOBER COMBAT

October anti-shipping strikes involved three days in particular. On the 5th Scouting Three damaged the destroyer *Minegumo*. On the 12th a pair of 2000-ton destroyers succumbed to joint air attacks – *Marakumo* to SBDs and Torpedo Eight, while Scouting Seventy-One and two other squadrons put under *Natsugumo*.

Thirteen days later Lt Cdr Eldridge and VS-71 combined with AAF P-39s and B-17s to sink the light cruiser *Yura*. That same day a destroyer was damaged as well.

On 26 October American and Japanese carriers clashed for the fourth time. The Imperial Navy and Army, in a rare attempt at strategic co-operation, launched a combined offensive to take Guadalcanal by sea and by land. US intelligence was aware of the enemy's intention, and aircrews were briefed on the night of the 25th, following an abortive search-strike. There was no doubt that the next day would bring combat.

A newly-winged combat aircrewman was Radioman 3rd Class David Cawley, assigned to Scouting Ten in *Enterprise*. The 18-year-old flier found a rough way to break into combat – the sanguinary Battle of Santa Cruz.

Cawley was roused at 0300 and reported to the VS-10 ready room an hour later. There he learned that he was assigned a sector search with his pilot, Lt(jg) K B Miller, and Lt(jg) Howard Burnett and Radioman R P Wynn. The two-SBD section launched into the early-morning sky with about 40 per cent cloud cover, bases at 1800 ft. Cawley takes up the narrative;

'We headed out to our assigned NW direction and settled to cruise speed at about 1200 ft. I had my guns out, safety on, and the cockpit open. It was cool and there was very good visibility under the puffy cumulus clouds.

'About 1.5 hours outbound, I noticed a very slight bump on the horizon nearly dead ahead. I notified Mr Miller on the intercom, and we agreed it had to be the top mast of some ship. I waved the other plane up and pointed. I estimate it was 30 miles or so. We both lowered our altitude until it was out of sight over the horizon, and we proceeded on for eight miles.

'Eventually we climbed up again and took a good look. Directly ahead of us about 12 to 15 miles was a beautiful enemy fleet: two *Kongo*-class battleships with the big pagoda masts. They were accompanied by about four cruisers and six to eight destroyers, headed south at about 20 knots.

'We quickly composed a contact report, and I turned on our radio transmitter and sent the contact by CW (continuous wave) twice. Of course *Enterprise* was maintaining radio silence and we didn't really expect an answer.

'Now we were only four to five miles from the Japanese battle force, and when I looked around, Mr Burnett was climbing away to starboard. We turned to follow him and started our climb. Each plane carried a 500-lb bomb. We continued our climb among rather built-up cumulus that extended to 10,000 ft. There was no sign of Japanese planes.

'When we reached 8500 ft, Burnett was about 2000 ft above us and about a mile north. He turned toward the enemy, due west, and I told Mr Miller, so we turned to time our attack with his. He was approaching the Japanese from their port quarter and we were just forward of the centre of their force on the port side. They hadn't changed course or speed all this time.

'The task force was still heading south in beautiful formation, and we were very close. When we were at an elevation of about 80 degrees, a heavy cruiser on our side turned toward us and started flashing a searchlight. It was obvious he wanted a recognition signal. Of course we couldn't provide one, so he kept signalling. Our dive flaps started to open and we armed our bomb.

'The big cruiser started firing all his guns at us, followed in moments by several other ships. I was standing up in the back cockpit, hanging onto my guns with one hand and leaning out, looking over the wing at the ships. I wondered where all those shells and AA projectiles were. Then the sky just exploded with every colour – grey, black, silver, blue and long trails of smoky phosphorous. One went off under our right wing and we were blown over on our back. A terrible loud *wham*, like being in a tin can someone hit was a shotgun. We dove away and closed our flaps and dropped our bomb. I don't know where it went.'

Both bombs fell near the cruiser *Tone*, which was unharmed.

Radioman 3rd Class David Cawley was an 18-year-old gunner assigned to Scouting Ten in October 1942. His first combat mission was a search flown with Lt(jg) K B Miller during the Santa Cruz engagement, in which his section found the Japanese battleship force. Cawley remained with *Enterprise* and flew a second tour, serving as Lt Cdr J D Ramage's rear--seat man in 1943-44. Cawley remained in the navy postwar, became an aviator, and retired as a commander (*David E Cawley*)

'The AA continued as we dove at very high speed clear down to 50 or 100 ft from the water, heading east. The battleships began shooting their main batteries at us. The big shells would hit the water very near and send up big geysers. We would take evasive action and they still came close. This went on until we were over the horizon and a full 15 miles away, and only the tops of their pagodas were visible.

'At last we were over the horizon and they stopped shooting. We checked with each other and determined we were both OK. We weren't so sure about the plane, but it seemed to run and handle alright. We couldn't see Burnett's plane.'

Miller and Cawley navigated back to the expected 'Point Option', but the task force, under Japanese attack, was miles away. Homing on the YE-ZB signal, they found a familiar silhouette and flew close aboard. It was *Hornet*, which immediately opened fire as Aichi D3A dive-bombers attacked. Evading the flak, Miller turned away and saw *Enterprise* emerge from a rain squall ten miles south.

Landing aboard after some five hours aloft, Miller and Cawley quickly learned they were far from safe. Almost immediately after their SBD was lowered to the hangar deck a Japanese bomb exploded aft of the elevator they had just ridden. Cawley was knocked to the deck by the force of the explosion, but was otherwise safe.

VOSE OVER *SHOKAKU*

Meanwhile, the US task force launched dive-bombers and torpedo planes against the Japanese carriers. While airborne, the American and Japanese strike groups passed one another – some Zeros roughly handled the *Enterprise* formation, but *Hornet's* formation remained relatively undisturbed until arriving in the target area. Leading 15 Bombing and Scouting Eight aircraft was VS-8's skipper, Lt Cdr W J 'Gus' Widhelm, widely regarded as one of the leading characters of US naval aviation. Bombing Eight's Lt J M 'Moe' Vose, another Midway veteran, recalled;

'We had no sooner taken off when my squadron was at 5000 ft and overhead passed the Japanese air group. There was no question in my mind as to the objective. Gus Widhelm and I joined our squadrons, passed directly over the Japanese cruiser group and continued on, all the while under Zero attack. Gus was hit in sight of the carriers, and landed almost in the middle of the disposition.'

Widhelm and his gunner were later rescued.

'I was first to dive. Widhelm's people had joined on mine, and I saw three hits on *Shokaku*. As we pulled out we were taking evasive action at wave top level, under continued Zero attack.

'The Zeros finally retired and we came in sight of the task force. Recognition procedures for an even day were to make left-hand turns, and dip the left wing twice. As we would do so, we would be met by a hail of anti-aircraft fire! This is understandable, as the force had been under severe attack. The *Hornet* was badly hit and unable to take us aboard, and although *Enterprise* was on fire forward with a bomb hit aft, we still recovered aboard. On landing, the aft elevator of *Enterprise* was jammed in the down position, so it was necessary to catch the number one wire. I can recall that yawning hole in the deck as I landed and released my tail hook.

'When we landed, my flight officer, Fred Bates, gave me a piece of charred wood from the flight deck of *Shokaku*, from my hit! It had blown into his cockpit on his way down.'

Both sides gave as good as they got in the running battle over *Shokaku*. Of 15 SBDs in Widhelm's formation, two were shot down and two aborted, while VB- and VS-8 claimed an equal number of shootdowns and actually bagged two. Vose led his squadrons to *Enterprise*, as *Hornet* had sustained mortal damage from enemy bombers and torpedo aircraft. A year later he took Bombing Seventeen into combat aboard *Bunker Hill* (CV 17) for the first combat deployment of the Curtiss SB2C Helldiver.

NOVEMBER CLIMAX

The month started badly for SBD squadrons, as VS-71's skipper, Lt Cdr John Eldridge, was lost in a storm on the 2nd. At age 39, he was one of the most experienced strike leaders in the 'Cactus Air Force', and the former *Wasp* flier was badly missed.

Dauntlesses and Avengers damaged two destroyers on 7 November as no fewer than 11 vessels sped down 'The Slot' bearing 1300 troops. Maj Joseph Sailer of VMSB-132 led a combined bombing-torpedo attack through heavy flak and numerous float fighters. *Takanami* and *Naganami* received significant damage, but the reinforcement proceeded. The next night more Japanese ships successfully landed troops, and a late attack on the 10th, again led by Sailer, achieved no results.

Sailer led a short, eventful combat life during 37 days at Guadalcanal in November-December. In that period he flew 26 missions totalling 63.6 hours, with flight times between 0.8 and 4.2 hours – the average was 2.5 hours. He led or participated in 19 strikes, resulting in 12 contacts from which he dropped nine bombs for six credited hits. Additionally, he flew five observation flights and three searches. His most intensive period of operations was 13-14 November during the 'Battle of The Slot' when he flew four sorties amounting to six or seven hours each day. Attacks on the battleship *Hiei* and cruiser *Kinugasa* were highlights of Sailer's Guadalcanal career.

Those frantic days of mid-November represented the peak of the Guadalcanal air campaign. On the 13th, aided by *Enterprise's* Air Group 10, Marine SBDs and TBFs finished off the floating wreck that was *Hiei*, the battleship having been badly damaged in Ironbottom Sound during the previous night's surface battle.

The next morning, Navy and Marine squadrons caught a cruiser force retiring from a bombardment of Henderson Field. The first attack was led by Maj Joseph Sailer with VMSB-132, and 2Lt R E Kelly expertly placed his half-ton bomb in *Kinugasa's* vitals, killing the captain and executive officer. Subsequent attacks by VB- and VS-10 aggravated the vessel's flooding, ignited fuel and worsened her list. The 10,500-ton cruiser sank less than three hours after being hit.

Shortly after *Kinugasa* demise, a VB-10 section attacked *Maya*, which shot down Ens P M Halloran. His SBD struck the main mast and impacted near the portside five-inch mount, where 37 sailors were killed in the crash and resulting fire. Her sister *Chokai* was damaged by VS-10, with flooding of some forward compartments.

In concert with VMSB-132 and 142, *Enterprise* aircraft also sank two other transports. Later that day, as the Japanese reinforcement group

Maj Joseph Sailer assumed command of VMSB-132 in March 1942 and led the squadron for the next nine months. Arriving at Guadalcanal in late October, he flew almost daily for five weeks, logging 25 missions and a dozen attacks, and established a reputation for leadership that marked him for eventual command of an air group. Sailer was the fourth Marine dive-bomber commander killed during the campaign when he was shot down by Zeros while attacking a destroyer on 7 December 1942. In the opinion of his squadronmates, 'Joe Sailer was the best dive-bomber pilot in the Pacific' (*Alex White*)

shrugged off its losses and continued down 'The Slot', land-based SBDs (mostly Marines) destroyed four more transports.

Four surviving ships – some already damaged from the unrelenting air attacks – beached themselves during the night. There, they were easy targets for Henderson Field aircraft.

The 14 November operations were the most intensive ever undertaken by SBD squadrons. During the day Navy and Marine Dauntlesses attacked more than a dozen ships, including four cruisers and a destroyer, and sank seven.

From August through to the climax of mid-November, the 'Cactus Air Force' sank 20 Japanese ships (fourteen transports, three destroyers, two cruisers and a share in the destruction of the battleship *Hiei* with surface units), while damaging 14 more (seven destroyers, four cruisers and three transports.)

DECEMBER DENOUEMENT

By December VMSB-132 was among the more experienced attack squadrons at Henderson Field. Maj Sailer's regular radioman-gunner was Cpl Howard Stanley, who had enlisted in the Marine Corps at age 17 already possessing a private pilot's license.

Sailer was flying with another rear seat man when, on the first anniversary of 'Pearl', he led a six-aircraft attack on Japanese destroyers off New Georgia, some 160 miles from Henderson Field. The CO was seen to hit his target, which slowed perceptibly, but Sailer's aircraft was extremely slow at very low level. The major radioed that his dive brakes would not retract, which would force him to make a water landing – the SBD would not long maintain level flight with the flaps open.

At that vulnerable moment Sailer's aircraft was attacked by a Mitsubishi F1M1 floatplane (later code named 'Pete'). From six o'clock high the Japanese fighter raked the Dauntless with 7.7 mm fire, and VMSB-132 aviators watched aghast as their CO rolled inverted and crashed into the water. Maj Joseph Sailer, age 35, and 20-year-old PFC J W Alexander were both killed in action.

By early 1943 Henderson Field was almost exclusively devoted to 'Cactus' Strike Command, the fighters having moved to another field a mile east. Three SBD squadrons were on the strength of Strike Command in June, rising to five in December as increasing pressure was brought against the Japanese naval-air complex at Rabaul, New Britain

THE 1942 BOX SCORE

During 1942, Dauntlesses sank, in whole or in part, six aircraft carriers, one battleship, three cruisers and four destroyers, plus one submarine in December 1941. The ships listed below grossed nearly 200,000 tons;

DD *Kikuzuki*	4 May 42	Tulagi
CVL *Shoho*	7 May 42	Coral Sea
(shared with TBDs)		
CV *Akagi*	4 Jun 42	Midway
CV *Kaga*	4 Jun 42	Midway
CV *Soryu*	4 Jun 42	Midway
CV *Hiryu*	4 Jun 42	Midway
CA *Mikuma*	6 Jun 42	Midway
CVL *Ryujo*	24 Aug 42	Eastern
(Shared with TBFs)		Solomons
DD *Asagiri*	28 Aug 42	Guadalcanal
DD *Marakumo*	12 Oct 42	Guadalcanal
DD *Natsugumo*	12 Oct 42	Guadalcanal
CL *Yura*	25 Oct 42	Santa Cruz
(Shared with USAAF)		
BB *Hiei*	13 Nov 42	Guadalcanal
(Shared with TBFs)		
CA *Kinugasa*	14 Nov 42	Guadalcanal
(Shared with TBFs)		

Other agencies of the US and USMC sank one battleship, one cruiser and eleven destroyers in this same period, while the USAAF accounted for four more DDs. Clearly, in the year after Pearl Harbor, the Dauntless proved itself to be the worst enemy of the Imperial Japanese Navy.

In the four carrier battles of 1942, SBD squadrons dropped about 183 bombs on nine enemy carriers, scoring roughly 40 hits – both US and Japanese records are contradictory or inexact. This 20 per cent hit ratio against the Dauntless' primary target contrasts with about 15 per cent against smaller ships such as cruisers and especially destroyers. The dusk strike against *Tanikaze* at Midway on 6 June is a prime example, as 40+ SBDs from six squadrons all missed the well-handled destroyer. So did two flights of B-17s, which dropped 79 more bombs for one near miss.

Additionally, SBDs sank 14 transports at Guadalcanal, although several of these were shared with other land-based Navy and USAAF aircraft.

SBD Squadrons (outside ConUS) – December 1942

VB-3	17 SBD-3	USS *Saratoga* (CV 3)
VS-6	18 SBD-3	USS *Saratoga* (CV 3)
VB-10	16 SBD-3	USS *Enterprise* (CV 6)
VS-10	16 SBD-3	USS *Enterprise* (CV 6)
VB-11	18 SBD-3	Hawaii
VS-11	18 SBD-3	Hawaii
VGS-26	8 SBD-3	USS *Sangamon* (ACV 26)
VGS-29	9 SBD-3	USS *Santee* (ACV 29)
VMSB-132	15 SBD-3	Guadalcanal

VMSB-142	20 SBD-3	Guadalcanal/Espiritu Santo
VMSB-233	18 SBD-4	New Caledonia
VMSB-234	18 SBD-4	New Caledonia
VMSB-241	17 SBD-3	Midway

Total - 208

In June 1943 AirSols had three SBD squadrons – by year end the figure had grown to five, and that number would further increase in 1944. Allied airpower provided the roof under which naval and amphibious forces advanced up the Solomons chain with a series of operations in the summer and fall of 1943: the Russells (21 February); New Georgia proper (30 June); and finally the big island of Bougainville (1 November).

At the time of the New Georgia operation, which included a half-dozen landings at various beaches, land-based bombers from Guadalcanal were still within range of their main targets. VB-11 and -21, with VMSB-144, were at 'Cactus', with Bombing Eleven being rare among SBD units in that it was part of a full land-based air group. Originally intended to relieve *Hornet's* 'hodge-podge' squadrons, Air Group 11 was denied carrier duty when the ship was sunk at Santa Cruz. However, the squadrons operated ashore from April through to June, and eventually deployed in the second Hornet (CV 12) in 1944-45 (see *Osprey Aircraft of the Aces 10 Hellcat Aces of World War 2* and *Osprey Combat Aircraft Helldiver Units of World War 2*, both by Barrett Tillman, for further details).

SBD Squadrons (outside ConUS) – June 1943

VB-3	18 SBD-3/4	USS *Saratoga* (CV 3)
VB-9	16 SBD-4	USS *Essex* (CV 9)
VB-11	18 SBD-3	Guadalcanal
VB-12	19 SBD-3	Hawaii
VB-13	17 SBD-3/4	USS *Saratoga* (CV 3)
VB-21	19 SBD-3	Guadalcanal
VB-22	19 SBD-3/4	Hawaii
VS-23	9 SBD-4	USS *Princeton* (CVL 23)
VC-26	9 SBD-3	Efate, New Hebrides
VC-28	9 SBD-3	Efate, New Hebrides
VMSB-132	45 SBD-3	Espiritu Santo
VMSB-141	21 SBD	Auckland, New Zealand
VMSB-142	37 SBD-3/4	Nandi and Efate
VMSB-144	21 SBD	Guadalcanal
VMSB-151	20 SBD	Funafuti and Samoa
VMSB-234	15 SBD-4	Nandi
VMSB-235	17 SBD	Midway
VMSB-236	18 SBD	Hawaii
VMSB-241	21 SBD-4	Tutuila, Samoa
VMSB-243	15 SBD	Johnston Island
VMSB-244	23 SBD	Midway

Total - 406

'BOMBING ELEVEN' AT GUADALCANAL

The intimate teamwork of pilot and gunner was crucial to the successful completion of the scout-bomber mission. Unusual among Navy and Marine Corps crews was the team of Lt Edwin M Wilson and Radioman Harry R Jespersen, who flew together at Guadalcanal in 1943 and later aboard USS *Hornet* (CV 12) in 1944-45. This rare long-term pairing resulted in a high degree of co-ordination both in SBDs and SB2Cs. Wilson, who retired as a rear admiral, recalled his gunner's contribution to their success a half century after the war;

'As a young 17-year-old aviation radioman third class, Harry Jespersen was assigned as my gunner when VB-11 was commissioned with Air Group 11 at NAS North Island, in San Diego, California, on 10 October 1942. Bombing Eleven was scheduled to go aboard *Hornet* (CV 8), but it was sunk in the Battle of Santa Cruz in October 1942. With no carrier for Air Group 11, our first combat tour was at Guadalcanal, flying from Henderson Field between 23 April and 9 August 1943. We made attacks on Munda, Vila, Vanga Vanga, Ringi Cove, Rekata Bay, Viri Harbour and Kahili, on Bougainville, and against Japanese ships. Jespersen proved to be very sharp, intelligent, and an outstanding radioman. He was also an accurate gunner.

'On 8 May Japanese destroyers were reported in Blackett Strait, and VB-11 was ordered to attack them. The weather was lousy – when it was my turn to dive, I pulled up over the solid overcast and circled for awhile. Finally, through a hole in the cloud cover, I saw a DD and dove on it. Being the only plane in the area, I saw lots of tracers, and holes appearing in my wings. I got a hit on the DD with my 1000-lb bomb, and as I was pulling out saw three loaded landing barges heading for shore. Low on the water, I went back and forth, strafing them with my .50 calibres until I ran out of ammo. Then I circled so Jespersen could fire his ".30s" at the soldiers, who were firing their rifles and pistols at us. We sank one barge and stopped the other two.

'Both out of ammo, we returned to Henderson Field low on fuel and with lots of holes in the plane. One big hole in my port wing made a strange whistling sound. The engine quit, out of fuel as I was landing.

'That night the coast watcher on Kolombangara reported that the main attack did little damage because of the overcast and low clouds, but later a lone plane hit a destroyer which sank, and strafed three barges loaded with Japanese "marines" (special naval landing force) headed for his island. That the barges did not make it made him very happy. Years later I found out the coast watcher was Australian Lt Reg Evans, and that the DD I hit was the *Oyashio*. A couple of months after I sank the DD, Reg Evans saved Lt Jack Kennedy and his crew of PT-109 on 7 August 1943.

Lt(jg) Edwin Wilson of Bombing Squadron Eleven poses with his assigned aircraft. VB-11 had expected to operate from USS *Hornet* (CV 8) in late 1942 or early 1943, but the ship's loss at the Battle of Santa Cruz in October forced a change of plans. The entire air group went to Guadalcanal in April 1943 and flew against Japanese bases and shipping until that summer. Wilson and his radioman-gunner, Harry Jespersen, remained together for VB-11's second deployment, flying SB2C Helldivers from the second *Hornet* (CV 12) in 1944-45
(Rear Adm Edwin H Wilson)

'VB-11 departed for the States on 1 August, but Strike Command wanted six planes and crews to remain, and I was put in charge. On 9 August we finally ended our "Carrier Appreciation Tour", boarding the Dutch freighter *Japara*. Sixteen days later we arrived in San Francisco and went on leave. By then Harry had received the Purple Heart for shrapnel wounds to one leg during a mission on 9 July 1943.

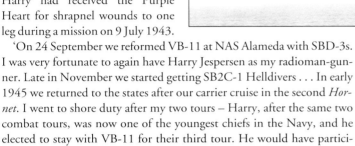

A VB-16 SBD-4 launches from *Lexington* on 23 April 1943

'On 24 September we reformed VB-11 at NAS Alameda with SBD-3s. I was very fortunate to again have Harry Jespersen as my radioman-gunner. Late in November we started getting SB2C-1 Helldivers . . . In early 1945 we returned to the states after our carrier cruise in the second *Hornet*. I went to shore duty after my two tours – Harry, after the same two combat tours, was now one of the youngest chiefs in the Navy, and he elected to stay with VB-11 for their third tour. He would have participated in the invasion of Japan if we had not fortunately dropped the atomic bombs on Japan, causing Tokyo to surrender.'

UPPER SOLOMONS ACTIONS

The largest SBD actions of late 1943 were two carrier strikes against Rabaul on 5 and 11 November. In the first, *Saratoga* and *Independence* (CVL 22) attacked warships in Rabaul Harbour. "Sara's" VB-12 Dauntlesses contributed to damage inflicted upon six cruisers and two destroyers, thus preventing interference with the Bougainville beach head.

On Armistice Day *Essex* (CV 9), *Bunker Hill* (CV 17) and *Independence* tried to finish off the cripples. A destroyer was sunk, but heavy opposition and poor weather hampered the strike groups. *Essex's* Bombing Nine was the only ship with SBDs, as *Bunker Hill* debuted the SB2C Helldiver, which would replace the Dauntless over the next eight months.

Meanwhile, by October about 100 Navy and Marine Corps SBDs were based at Munda to commence the land-based air offensive against Rabaul. The Marine units were VMSB-144 (Maj Frank E Hollar), VMSB-234 (Maj Harold B Penne) and VMSB-244 (Maj Robert J Johnson). Navy squadrons were largely independent units without a parent air group. Amphibious troops went ashore at Empress Augusta Bay on Bougainville's west coast on 1 November, with Dauntlesses and Avengers bombing and strafing ahead of the assault craft.

Close air support was increasingly important to the Marine air-ground team, and tests revealed that ordnance could be dropped extremely close to friendly troops under cover. Hundred-pound anti-personnel

The 'Bulldog Dive Bombers' of VMSB-233 on their way to bomb a Japanese airfield on Kolombangara, in the Solomon Islands. The lead aircraft is flown by Maj Claude J Carlson Jr, and is unusual in that it displays mission markers below the windscreen and the side number 77 repeated in black just below the rudder. Carlson commanded the squadron during May 1943, and then returned to the USA and organised a Hellcat nightfighter squadron VMF(N)-543. He was killed in an accident during July 1944

An SBD-3 of VMSB-243, flying either from Johnson Island or Hawaii, is seen during the latter half of 1943. The 'Flying Goldbricks' endured a long wait before reaching combat. Formed at Santa Barbara, California, in June 1942, the squadron deployed to Hawaii six months later, but was not committed to the Solomons campaign until November 1943. Subsequently, VMSB-243 participated in the Philippines campaign, before returning to the west coast of America in September 1945

bombs could normally strike 100 yards from riflemen, but as close as 75 yards in emergencies. The 'yard per pound' axiom held for 500 and 1000-lb bombs too, although half-ton weapons were occasionally dropped on Japanese positions within 300 yards of friendly troops.

Against Rabaul itself, a procedure had evolved by January 1944 involving specialised roles for SBDs and TBFs. While the Dauntlesses attacked precision targets such as anti-aircraft gun sites, the Avengers used their greater payloads on Rabaul's five airfields, and especially their runways. AirSols regarded neutralisation of Japanese fighter strips as paramount in achieving air supremacy over Rabaul, and the tactic worked.

Flying daily strikes for a period of months, SBDs and TBFs beat down the Imperial Navy forces while escorted by as many as 200 Corsairs and Hellcats. Meanwhile, US Fifth Air Force B-25s and A-20s added their weight to the effort. The last notable aerial combat of the campaign was fought on 19 February 1944 when an Allied strike of 145 aircraft was intercepted by an estimated 50 Japanese fighters. The next day Japan's surviving fighters retreated to Truk, and from then on Rabaul was increasingly regarded as a 'milk run'.

In the long campaign against Rabaul, Navy and Marine Corps squadrons flew some 19,000 of nearly 30,000 Allied sorties, while dropping 8500 tons of the 20,500-ton total.

The year's combat ended for the fast carriers with a strike against Kwajalein Atoll on 4 December. Heavily engaged was *Lexington's* Air Group 16, which encountered stiff aerial opposition over and around Roi Island. While VF-16 Hellcats claimed 20.5 kills and 2 probables, Lt Ralph Weymouth's SBD crews also found airborne hostiles. Lt(jg) A H Burrough splashed a 'Betty' bomber within five miles of the island, and shared another with an F6F. Weymouth himself, and Lt Cook Cleland, were each credited with a Zeke, while Dauntless gunners claimed four more aircraft confirmed and the squadron listed two additional probables. It was one of the most successful air-to-air actions ever recorded by an SBD squadron.

SBD Squadrons (outside ConUS) – December 1943

VB-1	36 SBD-5	Hilo, Hawaii
VB-5	36 SBD-5	USS *Yorktown* (CV 10)
VB-6	36 SBD-5	USS *Enterprise* (CV 6)
VB-9	36 SBD-5	USS *Essex* (CV 9)
VB-10	32 SBD-5	Puunene, Hawaii
VB-16	34 SBD-5	USS *Lexington* (CV 16)
VC-24	34 SBD-5	Munda (VB-98 from 15/12/43)
VC-35	9 SBD-5	USS *Chenango* (CVE 28)
VC-37	9 SBD-5	USS *Sangamon* (CVE 26)
VC-38	9 SBD-5	Munda, Solomons
VC-40	9 SBD-5	Munda, Solomons
VC-60	9 SBD-5	USS *Suwanee* (CVE 27)
VMS-3	6 SBD-5	St Thomas, Virgin Islands
VMSB-133	20 SBD-4	Johnston Island
VMSB-151	17 SBD-4	Wallis Island
VMSB-231	29 SBD-4/5	Midway
VMSB-235	21 SBD-4/5	Efate, New Hebrides
VMSB-236	29 SBD-4/5	Efate, New Hebrides
VMSB-241	23 SBD-4/5	Tutuila, Samoa
VMSB-243	22 SBD-4/5	Munda, Solomons
VMSB-244	27 SBD-4/5	Munda, Solomons
VMSB-245	21 SBD-5	Ewa, Hawaii
VMSB-331	18 SBD-5	Wallis Island
VMSB-341	16 SBD-5	Upolu, Samoa

Total - 538

Among the Navy squadrons committed to the Solomons offensive was VB-98, which flew from Munda, Bougainville and Green Island between November 1943 and mid-1944. Like many independent land-based squadrons not assigned to a carrier air group, VB-98 was built around a cadre of pilots taken from a composite squadron – in this case VC-24. The second unit to bear the VB-98 designation spent most of the war as part of a replacement air group (RAG) on the west coast

CENTRAL PACIFIC AND PHILIPPINES

Navy and Marine Dauntless squadrons in the Pacific faced a three-front war during 1943-44. Land-based units in the Solomons pursued the campaign against Japanese naval/air bases leading to Rabaul, New Britain, while Marine squadrons reduced, and then isolated, bypassed island garrisons in the Central Pacific. Finally, the new generation of aircraft carriers embarked upon a strategic offensive that would take SBDs from Rabaul to the Marianas.

It is at once ironic and instructive that the height of the SBD's wartime service occurred in the summer of 1944, just as the last two Dauntless squadrons were leaving carrier duty. By June, Bombing Ten in *Enterprise* and Bombing Sixteen in *Lexington* were the last two SBD units embarked in Task Force 58, but 18 other Navy squadrons and 11 Marine Corps units still flew the type outside the continental United States. Six were based in Hawaii, including bomber 'RAG' VB-100 at Barbers Point, where Curtiss SB2Cs were quickly replacing the last SBDs.

The high of 580 forward-deployed SBDs was largely due to 15 Navy scouting squadrons in the Hawaiian area, and the Central and Southwest Pacific. By year end only six of those remained, as their duty – searches and patrols – had largely been rendered unnecessary as the war pressed steadily westward.

SBD-5s of an unidentified carrier squadron return from a strike in late 1943 or early 1944. Empty bomb racks indicate that ordnance has been expended, but the fact that rear-seat guns are deployed means that interception by Japanese fighters remains a possibility

SBD Squadrons (outside ConUS) – June 1944

VB-10	21 SBD-5	USS *Enterprise* (CV 6)
VB-16	34 SBD-5	USS *Lexington* (CV 16)
VB-100	9 SBD-5	Barbers Point, Hawaii (RAG)
VB-305	24 SBD-5	Segi Field
VB-306	22 SBD-5	Torokina, Bougainville
VS-46	12 SBD-5	Pearl Harbour
VS-47	18 SBD-4	Johnston and Palymra Islands
VS-52	12 SBD-5	Roi, Marshalls
VS-53	18 SBD-5	Pearl Harbor
VS-51	14 SBD-5	Tutuila, Samoa
VS-54	16 SBD-3/4	Guadalcanal
VS-55	10 SBD-4	Espiritu Santo
VS-57	23 SBD-4	Noumea, New Caledonia
VS-58	10 SBD-4	Efate, New Hebrides
VS-64	10 SBD-5	Espiritu Santo
VS-65	15 SBD-4	Funafuti
VS-66	14 SBD-5	Tarawa Atoll
VS-67	10 SBD-3/4	Nandi
VS-68	10 SBD-4	Treasury Islands
VS-69	18 SBD-5	Pearl Harbour
VMSB-133	20 SBD-5	Ewa, Hawaii
VMSB-142	34 SBD-5	Ewa, Hawaii
VMSB-151	26 SBD-5	Engebi, Eniwetok Atoll
VMSB-231	22 SBD-5	Majuro Atoll
VMSB-235	19 SBD-4/5	Efate, New Hebrides
VMSB-236	22 SBD-5	Torokina, Bougainville
VMSB-241	21 SBD-5	Emirau
VMSB-244	18 SBD-5	Emirau
VMSB-245	20 SBD-5	Makin Island
VMSB-331	22 SBD-5	Majuro Atoll
VMSB-332	26 SBD-4/5	Midway

Total - 580

THE MARIANAS

Task Force 58 with 14 fast carriers arrived off the Marianas on 11 June 1944. Immediately launching a fighter sweep, Vice Adm Marc Mitscher's pilots began winning control of the air over the primary island bases on Guam and Saipan. Operation *Forager* was calculated not only to seize bases for long-range bombers, but to force the remainder of the Imperial Navy into combat.

The plan succeeded. Unable to allow B-29s within range of Tokyo, Naval General Headquarters directed Vice Adm Jisaburo Ozawa's First Mobile Fleet to disrupt the American landings at all costs. Ozawa sortied with nine carriers, setting the stage for the largest carrier battle of all time.

Mitscher's big-deck carriers operated SB2C squadrons and the last two SBD units still afloat. His flagship, *Lexington* (CV 16) embarked Lt Cdr Ralph Weymouth's VB-16, while *Enterprise* flew Lt Cdr J D Ramage's second-tour VB-10. *Forager* would be the SBD's last carrier operation.

The launch officer sends a Dauntless on its deck-run take-off from USS *Yorktown* (CV 10). Standing to the left of 'Fly One' is a sailor with a chalkboard containing last-minute tactical data for each pilot – usually an update on target location, or an adjustment in the ship's expected position upon the air group's return

The 'Marianas Turkey Shoot' occupied all of 19 June, with Hellcats winning outright air supremacy. American submarines sank two Japanese carriers, *Shokaku* and *Taiho*, but the Mobile Fleet remained out of Mitscher's range until late the following day. Then, on the afternoon of 20 June, Mitscher gave his famous order: 'Launch 'em.'

RAMAGE AT PHILIPPINE SEA

Lt Cdr James D Ramage was commanding officer of VB-10 during the First Battle of the Philippine Sea. His radioman-gunner was an old hand in *Enterprise*, as Radioman First Class David J Cawley had flown in VS-10 during the Santa Cruz battle of October 1942.

Ramage led 12 of his Dauntlesses with 17 other *Enterprise* aircraft in the evening attack on the Japanese carrier force on 20 June, the day after the epic Hellcat victory. He wrote;

'About 1 hour and 45 minutes out (260 nautical miles), I sighted a strike group to port in an attack situation. Beneath them I could see four oilers and several escorts. I broke radio silence, calling to Lt Van Eason, our torpedo leader, "85 Sniper from 41 Sniper. We will not attack. The Charlie Victors (CVs) are dead ahead".

'Radio discipline was not good. I could hear all sorts of completely unwarranted transmissions from over the target area. Well, at least the Japanese carriers were found.

'Cawley informed me that there were several Zeros high on our port quarter. Each time they commenced a run, Cdr WR "Killer" Kane nosed into them with his F6Fs and the Japanese would break off. They had decided to wait until our most vulnerable time – the point of roll into the attack. VB-10 did not dive from an echelon. Rather, during the high-speed run-in, the wingman would gradually drift back until the division leader rolled in. This preserved the V-formation as long as possible, per-

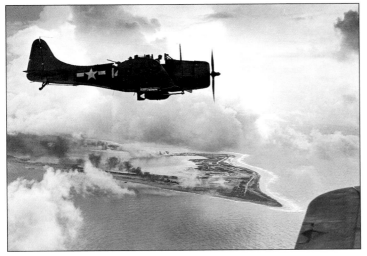

One of the most-published photos of the Pacific War was this profile of a Bombing Five aircraft over Wake Island on 5-6 October 1943. *Yorktown's* (CV 10) attack is well developed, as witnessed by fires burning at both ends of the island, but this Dauntless retains its 1000-pounder until the strike co-ordinator directs the section to a worthwhile target. This operation marked only the second time that US carriers had attacked the former American base

Carrying some of the most distinctive markings in Task Force 58, VB-9 aboard *Essex* (CV 9) used large white tail numbers rather than the more conventional fuselage and cowling numbers. This photo dates from late 1943, owing to the red border surrounding the national insignia. Bombing Nine participated in most of the major actions from Rabaul in November 1943 to the first Truk strike in February 1944

mitting the gunners to co-ordinate on an attack from the rear from either side.

'The Japanese fleet was easy to locate; there were black AA puffs over a wide area. Soon I could make out two carriers below and to port. It was to be just as we had briefed. I would take the closest carrier and Lt Lou Bangs' division would take the second. Eason's torpedo planes would split between the two. The TBFs were carrying four 500-lb bombs. The SBDs each carried one 1000-pounder. Half were general purpose and half were semi armour-piercing.

'As I rolled in I had a fine view of the carrier. I split my dive brakes at about 10,000 ft. Shortly thereafter I heard Cawley's twin ".30s" chattering, then I looked over to the right and, apparently within five feet of me, passing below was a Zero. My deceleration had thrown off his aim.

'My dive was a standard 70-degree attack. At about 8000 ft I opened up with my two .50-cal machine guns and saw the tracers going into the ship's forward elevator. Allowing for wind and target motion, I put the pipper on the bow of the carrier, which was steaming into the wind, and released at 1800 ft.

'I pulled out, easing down to about 300 ft, and was immediately taken under fire by all sorts of ships – battleships, cruisers and destroyers. Cawley yelled for me to look at the ship, which seemed afire from stem to stern. But there was so much stuff being thrown at us that I just couldn't look back. Cawley then began telling me to climb or descend, depending on where the AA was aimed. We pulled out to the east.

'As soon as I was clear of the Japanese outer screen, I started a gentle turn to the left at 1000 ft. It was about 1930 and beginning to get dark. Shortly I had six of my birds, then three more. Several Zeros were about to make runs on us, but Kane's fighters shot down four or five. After three orbits I knew we'd have to start back to TF-58. As I gave the hand signal indicating that we were squared away on our return course, I began to pick up all sorts of stragglers. As soon as they picked up my heading they added throttle and left us. They weren't gong to get stuck with the SBD's 150-knot max cruise speed!

'At 2120 Cawley had a good heading to the "Big E". The YE/ZB signals were in the correct sector. I figured we were about 30 miles out from Task Group 58.3, as I could see the loom of lights dead ahead. The panic was getting worse on the

The VB-16 crew of Lt Cook Cleland and Radioman W J Hisler established a reputation for aggressiveness among *Lexington* (CV 16) aircrews. Between them, the pilot and gunner were credited with at least three enemy aircraft shot down between December 1943 and June 1944. They flew the famous 'Mission Beyond Darkness' on 20 June, attacking a Japanese carrier and barely returning to the task force. After the war Cleland was closely linked with the Corsair, winning the Thompson Trophy Race in a modified Goodyear F2G in 1947 and 1949, and leading a Reserve F4U-4 squadron during the Korean combat embarked on USS *Valley Forge* during 1951-52

radio, and some blame must go to the excessive amount of lights on the ships. Some cruiser was firing star shells – just what we needed with a couple of hundred planes in the area. Our problem wasn't finding the force – that was a piece of cake. With everything including destroyers lighting up, it became a real mess. The hard part was finding a carrier amid all those lights.

'By now we had received a transmission to land on any deck available. I wasn't about to lose the integrity of my formation, letting individual planes mill around in confusion. At 2140 I brought the "Sniper" flight up *Enterprise's* starboard side and broke the first section into the landing pattern. Cawley said, "Skipper, it looks like a crash on the deck." I concurred, but knowing how fast the *Enterprise* crew worked, I hoped that by the time I came downwind the deck would be clear. I could see our LSO, Hod Proulx, giving a slow wave-off signal. As we went up the port side I saw real trouble on the flight deck – lights on and a plane on its back.

'At that time I called, "Sniper flight, our base has a foul deck. Pancake on any available base. This is 41 Sniper. Out".

'By this time the noise had subsided, but there were still too many lights. I finally located what I believed to be a light carrier, but just as I was getting squared away on it, I looked dead ahead maybe two miles and there was a big carrier. I was too high for a straight-in, so I elected to make a normal carrier pass. Cawley advised me that we were alone in the pattern and the landing was smooth. As I taxied out of the gear I received frantic "wing fold" signals from each plane director. They didn't realise that SBD wings don't fold! I finally got into a parking spot forward of the barriers when a flight deck man jumped on my wing, saying, "Get the hell out of here!" It was obvious that he was afraid of a plane jumping the barrier. Cawley and I ran into the island structure where I immediately asked, "What carrier?"

'"*Yorktown*", a crewman responded. My friend and squadronmate, Lt(jg) Don "Hound Dog" Lewis, and his gunner John Mankin, met us. We hadn't seen them since the ready room six hours before. It was a long day!'

BOMBING SIXTEEN OVER THE MOBILE FLEET

The VB-16 action report said in part;

'Fourteen VB planes broke up to initiate their dives in an easterly direction at approximately 1800. Dives were initiated at 11,500 ft at angles from 65 to 70 degrees. Releases were made from 2000 to 1400 ft and recoveries from 1300 to 800 ft. Dives were made in the face of extraordinarily intense AA fire of all descriptions from the enemy ships. At least one plane was harassed in its dive by enemy fighters.

'The first three planes, one carrying a 1000-lb GP bomb, the other two carrying 1000-lb SAPs, dove on the southern *Hayataka* class CV (this was a misnomer, as there was no *Hayataka* – she was probably *Hiyo*). The ship was manoeuvring violently, turning left from a course of 330 to 290. It was on a course of 290 moving downwind when hit . . . heavy black smoke immediately poured from the ship. The 4th and 5th planes also dove on this ship. The 6th plane dove on the other, northern CV. This SAP bomb missed by less than the width of the carrier's deck.

'The 7th, 8th and 9th planes dove on the southern CV. At this time it

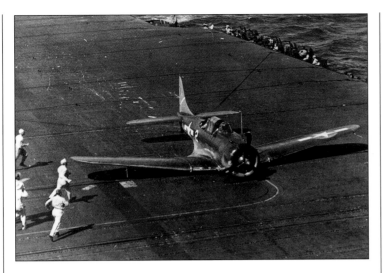

A VB-5 aircraft 'belly flops' onto *Yorktown's* flight deck after suffering landing gear failure on 22 February 1944. This event occurred five days after the two-day attack on the enemy fleet base at Truk Atoll, in the Caroline Islands – this operation was a major success for carrier aviation, resulting in the loss of 37 Japanese naval and merchant vessels of some 200,000 tons displacement

was smoking badly from previous hits . . . at least one of these bombs was a hit.'

Upon rejoining formation at low level, the *Lexington* SBDs were attacked by eight or more Zekes. One pressed its run on the plane of Lt(jg) J A Shields, who was killed with his gunner, Radioman C A LeMay. Both SBD squadrons lost a plane in water landings, and VB-16 jettisoned another following a crash landing, but the crews were rescued.

It was a close-run thing; VB-16's returning SBDs averaged just 24 gallons remaining while Bombing Ten – the last group to depart the task force – had 54 gallons, or enough for roughly one more hour.

PHASE OUT

The final SBD-6 rolled off the El Segundo assembly line in July 1944, and the Navy accepted its last 18 Dauntlesses the next month. A 'dash six' cost the US Government $29,000, compared to the prototype XBT-1 of 1934 which cost $85,000 to design and build. Noting the passing of a legend, *Time* magazine said, 'She had no bugs, no streaks of temperament; she was a thoroughly honest aircraft. She could take a frightful beating and stagger home on wings that sometimes looked like nutmeg graters'.

With the departure of Bombing Ten and Sixteen from the fast carriers, the SBD's primary contribution to the Allied cause came to an end. In 32 months of carrier combat, at least 62 carrier-based SBD pilots and 63 aircrewmen from ten ships had been killed in action, plus many others lost operationally. By far the greatest portion of combat losses – nearly half – were from the original Enterprise Air Group and Air Group 10. The breakdown was thus;

A Bombing Ten SBD-5 circles *Enterprise* whilst supporting the Emireau Island landings on 20 March 1944. While two CVEs protected battleships bombarding Kavieng on the tip of New Ireland, the 'Big E' was focused on Emireau, 90 miles to the northwest. Marines captured the island, which soon became an advance base for further operations in the reduction of the naval-air complex at Rabaul, New Britain

Lexington (CV 2)	VB-2, VS-2	5 pilots	5 aircrew
Saratoga (CV 3)	VB-3	1 pilot	1 aircrew
Ranger (CV 4)	VS-41, VB-4	2 pilots	1 aircrew
Yorktown (CV 5)	VB-5, VS-5, VB-3	11 pilots	11 aircrew
Enterprise (CV 6)	VB-6, VS-6, VB-10, VS-10	27 pilots	29 aircrew
Wasp (CV 7)	VS-71	0 pilots	1 aircrew
Hornet (CV 8)	VB-8, VS-8	2 pilots	2 aircrew
Essex (CV 9)	VB-9	2 pilots	2 aircrew
Yorktown (CV 10)	VB-5	6 pilots	5 aircrew
Lexington (CV 16)	VB-16	6 pilots	6 aircrew

THE DAUNTLESS 'AIR-TO-AIR'

On its first day in combat, the SBD suffered five losses to Japanese aircraft in exchange for one Zero destroyed – the A6M2 that collided with a VS-6 aircraft. Actual shootdowns of Japanese aircraft were also credited to Navy and USMC Dauntlesses during the course of the war, versus perhaps 43 SBDs known or thought lost to enemy aircraft. The large majority of those (39 by official count) were carrier-based in 1941-42.

The voluminous research of Dr Frank Olynyk has identified 135 of the 138 official SBD aerial victories, based on close scrutiny of squadron records.

At least 22 Navy SBD squadrons were credited with 94 aerial victories, largely during 1942. Victory credits were almost evenly divided between pilots and gunners, although at least five were attributed to squadron formations.

The greatest discrepancy is the number of aerial victories credited to Marine Corps SBD squadrons. Official figures are 22, which almost certainly reflects only the Guadal-

Eleven SBD-5s in formation after the strike on Palau of 30 March 1944. Over the next two days, the 11 fast carriers of TF-58 attacked Japanese bases in the western Carolines while amphibious forces landed at Hollandia, New Guinea. Three TBF squadrons mined Palau Harbor while SBDs and other aircraft claimed 28 ships sunk of 108,000 gross tons

'Thirty-Six Sniper' – an SBD-5 of Bombing Squadron Ten – is seen overhead *Enterprise* on 5 June 1944. At this time the Fifth Fleet was en route to the Marianas for the capture of Saipan. Fighter sweeps and bombing missions began on the 11th, and the two-day 'Marianas Turkey Shoot' took place on the 19th and 20th. It was the fifth, and last, carrier battle in which the SBD was involved – a record unmatched by any other American aircraft, although A6M Zeroes and D3A 'Vals' were engaged in every carrier duel of the war

canal claims – a similar number is attributed to land-based marine units in the central and upper Solomons battles of 1943-44.

Leading Navy SBD Squadrons, Air-to-Air

VS-2	*Lexington* (CV 2)	13.5
VS-10	*Enterprise* (CV 6)	11
VB-16	*Lexington* (CV 16)	10.5
VB-2	*Lexington* (CV 2)	8
VS-5	*Yorktown* (CV 5)	6
VS-6	*Enterprise* (CV 6)	6
VS-71	*Wasp* (CV 7)	5

Leading Navy SBD Pilots

Lt(jg) John Leppla	VS-2	4
Lt(jg) William E Hall	VS-2	3
Lt(jg) Stanley W Vejtasa	VS-5	3 (+8 in F4Fs)
Lt Cook Cleland	VB-16	2
Lt(jg) William E Johnson	VS-10	2
Ens RF Neely	VS-2	2
Lt(jg) Chester V Zalewski	VS-71	2

Leading Navy SBD Gunners

ARM2/c John Liska	VS-2, VS-10	4
ARM2/c WC Colley	VS-10	2

The top scoring Navy SBD crew was Lt(jg) John Leppla and his gunner, Radioman 3rd Class John Liska, with seven claims in the Coral Sea battle (four by the pilot). Lt(jg) W E Hall was credited with three enemy aircraft while defending *Lexington* on 8 May 1942, and Ens R F Neely claimed two – Hall received a Medal of Honor for continuing to fight after being wounded by Zeros. An accomplished *Yorktown* pilot, Lt(jg) S W 'Swede' Vejtasa, also was credited with three aircraft during the low-level anti-torpedo plane patrol on the 8th. During the war, three other Navy SBD pilots also claimed two shootdowns.

Leppla shortly transferred to VF-10 in *Enterprise*, but was killed during the Santa Cruz battle of 26 October. Liska added a fourth victory while flying with Scouting Ten in the same engagement. VS-10 claimed seven Zeros and a Kate in that battle, while *Hornet* SBDs claimed five.

Wasp's Dauntlesses stole a march on the carrier's two fighter squadrons, with seven actual shootdowns before the F4Fs notched their first. VS-71's Lt(jg) R L Howard shot down a Rabaul-based A6M2 fighter over Tulagi on 8 August 1942 at the start of the Guadalcanal campaign, while Lt(jg) Chester Zalewski and ARM3/c L H Faast claimed two Aichi E13A float-

This VB-16 aircraft, seen over Saipan on 15 June 1944, carries a full loadout of a 1000-lb bomb on the centreline rack and a 250-pounder under each wing. Bombing Sixteen had more consistent markings than most carrier-based units of the period, with a squadron emblem on the engine access panel and the tally of strike missions represented by stencilled bombs below the windscreen. The assigned pilot and gunner's names were stencilled below the respective cockpits as well. Number 18 is probably a replacement aircraft, as only five mission markers are displayed, and the fuselage star is the small-diameter version placed well aft. The squadron's older aircraft had large diameter stars immediately aft of the gunner's position, as per the 1943 version which originally lacked the horizontal bars

planes ('Jakes') on the 25th. That same day a VS-71 flight combined to splash a large Kawanishi H8K1 flying boat ('Emily'). Scouting Seventy-Two also downed a 'Jake' and another 'Emily' during the month. All of these claims are substantiated by Japanese records, and *Wasp's* fighter pilots insisted that the SBD pilots 'tend to their own business'!

Aerial combat for carrier-based SBD crews diminished drastically after 1942. During 1943 they claimed 13 victories against two losses to Japanese aircraft, and during the first half of 1944 (prior to SBDs leaving carrier service) the exchange was 5-2.

Over the Japanese fleet on 20 June 1944, VB-16 claimed 2 kills and 13 damaged – all but one of these claims were made by gunners. This was by far the largest aerial combat in which SBDs were involved, as VB-10 was intercepted by ten or more Zekes.

Thirteen Marine Corps SBD squadrons were credited with 41 enemy aircraft, including 21.5 at Guadalcanal. Of the Marine claims, 35 went to gunners, seven to pilots and three were collaborative kills.

Leading Marine Corps SBD Squadrons, Air-to-Air

VMSB-132	Solomons	6
VMSB-231	Solomons	6
VMSB-236	Solomons	5
VMSB-241	Midway, Solomons	5 (+2 in SB2Us)
VMSB-141	Solomons	4
VMSB-233	Solomons	4

By comparison, 'Leatherneck' TBF Avengers claimed 23.5 shoot-downs.

Marine Corps Pilots

1st Lt John McGuckin	VMSB-132	2

Leading Marine Corps SBD Gunners

Sgt Wallace Read	VMSB-231	3
Sgt Virgil S Byrd	VMSB-231	2

Squadron Variations

A short-lived concept in USMC aviation at this time was the 'bombing-fighting' squadron (VMBF). The designation shortly preceded the VBF units established in Navy carrier air groups when more fighters were

Lt Cdr James D Ramage was widely known in Task Force 58 as 'Jig Dog,' the popular, aggressive skipper of VB-10. Ramage, and Lt Cdr Ralph Weymouth of VB-16, led the last two carrier-based SBD squadrons, as the other five 'big-deck' carriers embarked the SB2C-1 Helldiver, which fully replaced the Dauntless in the Fast Carrier Force at the end of July 1944. Owing to heavy SB2C losses on 20 June, Ramage and Weymouth suggested to Vice Adm Marc Mitscher that SBDs be reissued to carrier bombing squadrons, but Dauntless production ended in July, and no further spare parts were forthcoming (*R L Lawson*)

Maj James Otis in B-1 leads a procession of VMSB-331 aircraft taxying for a mission against Mille Atoll on 22 August 1944. Otis commanded the 'Doodlebug Squadron' during most of its tenure at Majuro, in the Marshall Islands, where it began bombing bypassed Japanese bases in February 1944. The squadron was redesignated VMBF-331 from October to December, but then reverted to the original scout-bomber designation for the remainder of hostilities

Another VMSB-331 SBD over Majuro in mid-1944, flown by Capt Ernesto Guisti. The aircraft's previous squadron number, 26, has been painted over in dark blue on the tail while the current number 12 is placed on the fuselage. Many of the 4th Marine Air Wing squadrons in the Marshalls had non-standard markings owing to the frequent transfer of aircraft from unit to unit

VMSB-243 SBD-6 was photographed on 25 October 1944 at Emirau. Its official caption read; 'Lt Heublein won't let Gretchen (on the wing) go up with him in an SBD – he's afraid she'll dive out from 3000 ft – but she knows her dive-bombers from wing tip to wing tip. She runs up and down the wings until the sun on the aluminium gets so hot on her feet that she has to jump to the ground or into the cockpit'

required to meet the increasing *kamikaze* threat in early 1945. During December 1944 at least four Marine squadrons bearing the new designation were deployed in the Central Pacific with a mixture of fighters and dive-bombers: VMBF-231 and -331 each had 24 F4U-1Ds and two SBD-5s at Majuro, as did VMF-113 and -422 at Engebi.

The VMBF appellation was also borne by some 'pure' fighter squadrons wholly equipped with Corsairs, evidently in an attempt to identify the units' missions (i.e., air-to-ground), rather than reflect their assigned aircraft. In any case, the concept predated by nearly 40 years the VMFA designation used by F-4 Phantom II and then F/A-18 Hornet squadrons of the early 1980s.

SBD Squadrons (outside ConUS) – December 1944

VB-100	7 SBD-5	Barbers Point, Hawaii
VS-46	12 SBD-5	Pearl Harbor
VS-47	17 SBD-4	Palmyra and Johnston
VS-52	13 SBD-5	Roi
VS-53	18 SBD-5	Pearl Harbor
VS-66	15 SBD-5	Tarawa Atoll
VS-69	18 SBD-6	Pearl Harbor
VMSB-133	23 SBD-6	Torokina
VMSB-142	20 SBD-6	Emirau
VMSB-151	24 SBD-5	Engebi, Eniwetok Atoll
VMSB-236	23 SBD-6	Torokina
VMSB-241	22 SBD-6	Munda
VMSB-243	25 SBD-6	Emirau
VMSB-244	25 SBD-5	Green Island
VMSB-245	24 SBD-6	Majuro Atoll
VMSB-341	21 SBD-6	Green Island
VMSB-343	10 SBD-5	Midway

Total - 317

PHILIPPINES

Marine Air Group 12 arrived in the Philippines in early December 1944 with four F4U squadrons and an F6F nightfighter unit. They were followed by another fighter group, MAG-14, in January.

The first 'Leatherneck' dive-bombers committed to the campaign were four SBD squadrons of MAG-24, which arrived at Mangaldan, at the end of Lingayen Gulf, in late January 1945. Working up at Bougainville, the Marine aviators had trained in close air support techniques with the Army's 37th Infantry Division, learning how best to co-ordinate air and ground assets via a sophisticated radio communications network with forward controllers. Including the three squadrons of MAG-32, the

Luzon-based Marines had 174 Dauntlesses ashore by the end of January. Their first loss occurred on the 28th when an aircraft and crew of VMSB-133 succumbed to ground fire.

The prime objective of the Luzon campaign was Manila, the Philippine capitol. Beginning in the early hours of 1 February, the First Cavalry Division struck southward with almost continuous support of nine SBDs overhead, operating in relays. Scouting ahead, seeking the most direct route and avoiding Japanese strongpoints when possible, the Marines expedited the rush to liberate prisoners of war in the notorious Santo Thomas camp.

When necessary, the Marines' 'steamroller dive-bombing' ability was capable of an awesome concentration of ordnance. Missions of 80 aircraft from as many as five squadrons could obliterate most targets assigned, as when soldiers found every bomb hit contained within a grid measuring 200 by 300 yards. Supporting the 66-hour thrust to Manila, MAG-24 and -32 earned unstinting respect of friend and foe alike.

Among the dive-bomber pilots engaged in the campaign was Lt Frank McFadden of VMSB-236. He logged more than 1000 hours in SBDs, including combat in the Solomons and Philippines. His conclusion, 'A more reliable aircraft has never been built.'

Marine aviators on Luzon typically flew 13 to 16 missions per month for an average of 40 hours flight time, including non-combat sorties. McFadden's record was typical, his logbook for 1945 showing;

February	14 missions for 35.3 hrs
March	18 missions for 41.2
April	17 missions for 39.8
May	16 missions for 42.7
June	9 missions for 22.4

This tallied up to give him 74 flights for 181.4 hrs, during which he was involved in 65 strikes.

Champion dive-bomber pilot of the US Marine Corps was Maj Elmer G Glidden Jr (left), who commanded VMSB-231 from September 1942 to September 1944. Beginning his combat career with VMSB-241 at Midway, Glidden then commanded the 'Ace of Spades' squadron as part of the 'Cactus Air Force' at Guadalcanal. In addition to his 27 missions in 1942, Glidden's tour in the Marshalls brought his wartime total to 104 – more combat dives than any other Marine scout-bomber pilot. His radioman-gunner for all 77 missions in the Marshalls was M/Sgt James Boyle

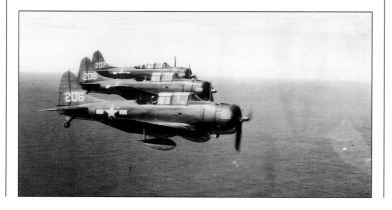

VMSB-236 Dauntlesses are probably seen being ferried from Bougainville to Luzon, as evident by the lack of ordnance and presence of two underwing drop tanks. The squadron spent the last two years of the war flying against Japanese bases in the Solomons area and the Philippines, having logged the first dive-bombing attack against Bougainville in September 1943. Subsequent bases were Torokina, Green Island and finally Luzon, beginning in January 1945. The unit was disestablished in the Philippines on 1 August 1945, two weeks before the cessation of hostilities (*John M Elliott via Peter B Mersky*)

The No 2 aircraft of VMSB-231 on patrol over Majuro anchorage in early 1944. This Dauntless displays the squadron's typical markings of the period – 'Ace of Spades' emblem ahead of the windscreen, the pilot's tally of 23 bombing missions, and the individual side number all rendered over the tri-colour camouflage scheme. The presence of only destroyers and destroyer tenders in the lagoon testifies to the 'backwater' nature of the sea war at this time, although Marine squadrons were flying almost daily missions against Japanese bases in the area

The Marine dive-bomber squadrons in the Philippines operated in what would later be termed a 'permissive environment'. Japanese airpower was crushed by February, the Marine Corps only claiming 75 shootdowns during six months in the islands.

Supporting the Army in the Philippines, McFadden recalled;

'We used to fly out of Dagupan south to large rice paddies on the north and east sides of Manila. We would land, be taken to forward positions on the line, observe infantry operations, be given targets, go back to our planes, take off, climb to 12,000 to 14,000 ft and dive-bomb assigned targets!'

The SBD's famous ruggedness was demonstrated convincingly to McFadden, who recalled a Valentine's Day 'present' from a Japanese flak battery;

'I was flying a strike at Fort McKinley, near Manila, on 14 February 1945 when I was hit by AA fire from Neilson Field. I flew the plane back to base at Dagupan, which is near the Lingayen Gulf, on Luzon. The stall speed with this damage, with wheels down, was 125 knots. I made my approach at 140, and the landing was successful.'

Upon investigation, the pilot found he could stand inside the hole made in his horizontal stabiliser.

Maj Gen Verne Mudge, commanding the First Cavalry Division, attested the support received from 'The Diving Devil Dogs of Luzon'. He wrote;

'The marine dive-bomber pilots are well qualified for the job they are doing, and I have the greatest confidence in their ability. On our drive to Manila I depended solely on the Marines to protect my left flank from the air against possible Japanese counter-attack. The job they turned in speaks for itself. We are here.'

Supporting that view, Maj Gen Charles Muller of the 25th Infantry Division said;

Luzon-based SBDs of the 1st Marine Aircraft Wing were instrumental in supporting Army troops during the drive on Manila. This SBD-6 prepares for take-off with a 500-lb bomb beneath the fuselage and 100-pounders on the wing racks, a typical loadout for close air support missions. The 1st Wing consisted of Marine Air Groups 12, 14, 24 and 32, of which the latter two each operated three SBD squadrons. MAG-12 and -14 also controlled seven F4U squadrons and an F6F-5N nightfighter unit

75

The Dauntless was rugged! 1st Lt FH McFadden of VMSB-236 flew 65 strikes in the Philippines, but the most memorable was a mission near Manila on 14 February 1945. The squadron attacked Nielsen Field and encountered intense anti-aircraft fire, with McFadden's aircraft taking a direct hit from an explosive shell. After recovery from his dive, he found the SBD stalled at 125 knots, so he made his landing approach at 140 instead of 90! He is seen here standing in the hole made in his horizontal stabiliser by the shell after safely returning to Dagupan Airfield
(*F H McFadden via Doug Champlin*)

'There is no way to measure factors in the success of the operation against Balete Pass. The dive-bombers hit targets that were unreachable by artillery and speeded up the advance toward the final objective.'

From January to July 1945, MAG-24 lost 12 officers and 18 enlisted men in combat, nearly all of whom were SBD crews. MAG-32, operating ashore for nearly as long, lost six officers and six enlisted men from headquarters and the SBD squadrons. Another 16 Dauntless personnel from both groups died of non-combat causes.

As of July 1945, only a half-dozen Marine squadrons with 144 SBD-6s still flew Dauntlesses in the Pacific. All were engaged in Philippine operations, where the majority were disestablished that month. MAG-24 stood down VMSB-133 and -241 on 16 July, as Col Warren E Sweetser paid tribute to the SBD crews at Titcomb Field, near Malabang, on Mindanao. The group's last 24 Dauntlesses were then flown to Cebu, where the navy disposed of them.

MAG-32's SBD squadrons stood down two weeks later, leaving the Helldiver as the Leathernecks' only combat dive-bomber. 'The Beast' had finally supplanted its 'obsolete' predecessor at the very end of World War 2, but it had taken the entire duration of that global conflict to do so.

SBD Squadrons (outside ConUS) – July 1945

VMSB-133	24 SBD-6	Cotobato, PI
VMSB-142	24 SBD-6	Zamboanga, PI
VMSB-236	24 SBD-6	Zamboanga, PI
VMSB-241	24 SBD-6	Cotobato, PI
VMSB-243	24 SBD-6	Zamboanga, PI
VMSB-341	24 SBD-6	Zamboanga, PI

Total - 144

Land-based US Navy scouting squadrons flew SBDs throughout the Pacific during 1943-44. These VS-51 aircraft were photographed during work-ups in Hawaii prior to deployment to Samoa in June 1944, where they flew routine searches and anti-submarine patrols. They are readily identifiable as land-based owing to the large pneumatic tailwheels in contrast to the smaller-diameter hard rubber wheels used on carrier-based SBDs

BANSHEES AND FOREIGN DAUNTLESSES

O n the other side of the globe, the Anglo-American invasion of North Africa began the week before the climax at Guadalcanal. US troops went ashore in French Morocco on 8 November 1942, supported by four carriers. *Ranger* and two escort carriers embarked 36 SBDs, while another CVE operated Avengers.

VS-41	18 SBD-3	USS *Ranger* (CV 4)
VGS-26	9 SBD-3	USS *Sangamon* (ACV 26)+9 TBFs
VGS-29	9 SBD-3	USS *Santee* (ACV 29) +8 TBFs
VGS-27	TBF-1	USS *Suwannee* (ACV27)

All 18 VS-41 SBDs launched from *Ranger* on the morning of 8 November, bound for Casablanca. Taken under AA fire over the harbour, they radioed the warning call, 'Batter up', and received permission to attack with 'Play ball'! Their primary target was the moored Vichy French battleship *Jean Bart*, named after the 17th century privateer. One Dauntless was shot down and three damaged during repeated sorties that saw most *Ranger* pilots fly four missions during the day.

About 90 minutes later a French naval unit sortied, causing concern for Allied shipping offshore. The squadron of destroyers (erroneously thought to include one or two cruisers) closed to about four miles of the

Supporting Operation *Torch* (the invasion of French North Africa), VS-41 flew SBD-3s from *Ranger* during November 1942. Seen on an anti-submarine patrol over troop transports bearing American assault forces, this Dauntless was on the lookout for Vichy French submarines as well as German U-boats. Of note is the absence of the yellow ring around the fuselage star which identified friendly aircraft to Allied ships and aircraft. Curiously, Vichy French aircraft also sported distinctive yellow markings at that time

transport group, but intense strafing by F4Fs held them up. In the lull *Ranger* SBDs and *Suwannee* TBFs attacked, claiming three hits, although one Dauntless fell to flak. Slowed by air attacks, the French warships were delayed in their task and finally undertaken by surface gunfire.

That morning involved certainly the most ironic event of Operation *Torch* – a brief combat occurred between a *Santee* SBD and a Vichy DB-7, which saw two Douglas aircraft shooting at each other! This fratricidal episode ended without result on either side.

Another veteran of *Torch* was VC-29, embarked in USS *Santee*, which was one of the escort carriers assigned to anti-submarine warfare in the Atlantic. Originally an 'escort scouting' unit (VGS-29), the squadron was redesignated a composite squadron in March 1943. These SBD-5s, photographed in late 1943, are being respotted forward on the flight deck after recovery. Their unusual markings are the full legend reminiscent of prewar practise – i.e. 29C22 – but the individual aircraft numbers are rendered in twice the size, and in white

Bombing Squadron Four's SBD-5s parked forward on *Ranger's* flight deck with VT-4 TBF-1s circa late 1943. Air Group Four attacked Axis-controlled shipping north of the Arctic Circle in Operation *Leader* during October of that year, sinking five ships and damaging several more near Bodø, in Norway. Two SBDs were shot down, with one crew lost and another captured

Marine Scouting Squadron Three (VMS-3) flew a variety of aircraft in the Caribbean Sea until disestablished in the summer of 1944. These five SBD-5s bear the attractive Atlantic colour scheme of flat insignia white overall with scalloped sea grey upper surfaces. At the end of 1943 the squadron listed six Dauntlesses at St Thomas, in the US Virgin Islands

Relatively little occurred for the SBDs on the second day of *Torch*, most of the Dauntless action occurring in the south, off Safi, where *Santee's* VGS-29 flew repeated anti-submarine patrols. However, during overland missions in support of ground forces two SBDs sustained AA fire, with one pilot and a gunner being wounded.

On 10 November VS-41 returned to finish off *Jean Bart*, with two of nine bombs scoring hits. A follow-up strike of seven SBDs went after El Hank's troublesome AA battery with 500-lb bombs.

The lone entry in the SBD's log book for aerial combat outside the Pacific occurred on the 10th. Ens Donald A Pattie of VGS-29 off *Santee* was leading a reconnaissance mission when his wingman's SBD was damaged by ground fire. Continuing alone, Pattie eluded three Vichy fighters and descended through a cloud layer to emerge over Chichaoua Airfield, near Marakesh. The runway was lined with fighters and twin-engine bombers as he related in his memoir, *To Cock a Cannon*;

'I saw one of the planes (a US-built DB-7) starting to take-off. It was necessary to stop him in a hurry as my SBD would be no match for his speed and power. Whipping around in a run from above, my rear gunner was instructed to shoot up as many of the parked planes as possible while I concentrated on the one taking off.

'It was shades of World War 1. SBDs had two forward-firing .50 calibre guns in the engine cowling . . . synchronised to fire through the propeller. As I came in, picking him up in my sights, I squeezed the trigger and cut a path of bullets right through the cockpit.

'After another pass at the parked planes the place was coming alive like a bee hive so I figured I better make tracks while I still could. Climbing up through the overcast, I broke radio silence to notify the ship of the location and headed for home.'

Pattie noted the irony of the situation in which two Douglas aircraft were pitted against one another. Nearly three years later, whilst commanding VT-23 aboard the light carrier *Langley* (CVL 27), Pattie led the US Navy's only night torpedo attack of the war.

Late on 10 November a mixed *Sangamon* formation was directed toward a French armoured column between Rabat and Port Lyautey. In one of the largest missions of the short campaign, a dozen VGS-6 SBDs and TBFs, escorted by ten F4Fs, conducted very low-level attacks to get at the vehicles in a grove of trees. Return fire was heavy, but all the CVE aircraft returned to the ship.

Finally, on the morning of the 11th, a *Santee* SBD and one F4F attacked Marrakech airfield, claiming three aircraft burned on the ground. By the end of the operation the American air groups were so depleted from losses and damage that several single-aircraft missions were flown. The cease-fire agreement went into effect that morning – appropriately on the 24th anniversary of Armistice Day.

However, surviving SBDs were not allowed much rest, as German U-boats arrived to replace the French submarines. One transport was sunk, while three carriers and a cruiser were attacked on the 12th.

In all, nine SBDs were lost to combat and operational causes during *Torch*, including four from *Santee's* VGS-29. The next Dauntless event against the western Axis would take place in far different circumstances.

Nearly a year after *Torch*, in October 1943, *Ranger* remained in the Atlantic with many of the same aircrews still aboard. Temporarily joining the British Home Fleet, the veteran carrier was assigned an antishipping strike against the German-occupied port of Bodø, in Norway. Above the Arctic Circle, Bodø was a remote, but significant, enemy port considered worthy of attack. Thus was born Operation *Leader*.

On 4 October, *Ranger* launched two strikes beginning with 20 SBD-5s, 150 miles offshore. Hunting along the rocky coast, Bombing Four crews spotted an 8000-ton freighter and hit her with two bombs. Further into the mission, Lt Cdr Gordon O Klinsmann led his divisions down on a tanker and transport, escorted by a destroyer. Six SBDs attacked, claiming hits on both ships, one of which grounded.

The balance of the strike force proceeded to Bodø Harbour, with four pair of SBDs each selecting a target. During the attack Lt(jg) C A Tucker and his gunner were killed by flak and another Dauntless ditched in the harbour and its crew captured.

The second launch comprised ten TBFs with escorts, and cost one Avenger shot down. Results of the mission were five ships sunk or destroyed and four seriously damaged.

WAIL OF THE BANSHEE

The US Army Air Forces flew A-24s in combat more than is generally known. In 1941 the AAF obtained 78 SBD-3s, designated A-24-DE (for Douglas) and named Banshee. The SBDs and A-24s alternated on the El Segundo, California, production line, with the Banshee's main external difference being a large pneumatic tailwheel and absence of the tail hook, although the hook fairing remained. At that time, the Army envisioned the Banshee as an operational trainer to fill the gap before other types arrived, notably the Curtiss A-25 and Vultee A-31 Vengeance.

However, the worsening situation in the Pacific caused shipment of the 27th Bomb Group's (BG) 52 Banshees to the Philippines. The aircrews had already arrived but the A-24s were still en route when war erupted, requiring diversion to Australia. There, they were delivered to the 91st Bomb Squadron, which sent a dozen aircraft to the defence of Java. Repeated sorties against Japanese beach heads failed to prevent enemy landings, and air superiority quickly passed to the Japanese. Badly outnumbered and out-performed, the A-24s were soon overwhelmed.

The balance of the shipment was taken over by the 8th BG, which deployed to Port Moresby, New Guinea. Their worst mission occurred on 29 July 1942 when seven aircraft intent on bombing Buna were intercepted by Zeros, which shot down five of their number. A-24s largely reverted to non-combat use for a year soon after this episode.

A prewar publicity photo of an A-24 nosing into a dive. Although minus ordnance, this Banshee represents the US Army Air Corps' minimal dive-bombing capability as of 1941. With the emphasis placed on multi-engine strategic bombers, the USAAC largely overlooked dive-bombers in its operational planning until Luftwaffe success demonstrated the combat value of such aircraft in land warfare. Studies demonstrated that twin-engined types such as the Douglas A-20 were limited to 30-degree attacks, reinforcing the impetus toward two-seat dive-bombers (*René Francillon*)

Despite an initial poor showing under adverse conditions, the Banshee remained in production. Ninety more A-24s were ordered in 1942, as were 170 A-24As (SBD-4). Throughout 1943, 615 A-24Bs (SBD-5s) were built at Douglas' new Tulsa, Oklahoma, factory, bringing total Banshee production to 875.

Although ten AAF groups flew A-24s after mid-1942, only two units logged additional combat. The 407th BG launched a mission against Japanese-occupied Kiska, in the Aleutians, in August 1943 but by then the island had been abandoned.

Factory-fresh A-24Bs delivered at Douglas Aircraft Company's plant in Tulsa, Oklahoma, probably circa December 1943. By that date the plant had built 615 dive-bombers for the Army, averaging 68 per month. Combined with 78 SBD-3s diverted from Navy orders, and 90 more built for the Army at El Segundo, California, Banshee production totalled 783 aircraft (*Rene' Francillon*)

Assigned to the Seventh Air Force, the 531st BS (Dive) in Hawaii was sent to the Gilbert Islands in 1943. Redesignated a fighter-bomber unit, the 531st flew alongside P-39s in conditions of US air supremacy. Beginning in December of that year, Makin-based Banshees attacked Japanese bases and shipping at Mille and Jaluit atolls, a process that continued into the spring of 1944. Subsequently, the 531st received P-40s and, ultimately, P-51s for long-range escort missions from Iwo Jima.

THE KIWI CONNECTION

The Royal New Zealand Air Force (RNZAF) had just one dive-bomber unit in World War 2, namely No 25 Sqn, flying Dauntlesses in 1943-44.

Formed at Seagrove, near Auckland, on 31 July 1943, No 25's commanding officer was Sqn Ldr T J MacLean de Lange, who later rose to the rank of air commodore. Originally equipped with nine SBD-3s from Marine Air Group 14, de Lange had 12 two-man crews and a few main-

Banshees saw limited combat in the Marshall Islands beginning in late 1943, attacking bypassed Japanese bases. The most frequent targets were Mille and Wotje, where enemy facilities remained until the end of the war. This aircraft, 42-54459, taxies behind a 'follow me' jeep on Makin Island as the radioman-gunner stands on the wing to watch for traffic hazards. The centreline fuel tank indicates that the A-24 is embarked upon a patrol rather than an offensive sortie (*Rene' Francillon*)

tenance specialists, but his aircraft were delivered in poor condition. At that time most Marine Air Groups had centralised maintenance, which was administratively simpler than squadron assignments because aircraft could be drawn from the group pool for operations. However, because the aircraft did not 'belong' to any squadron, maintenance quality tended to suffer. Therefore, a week passed before No 25 Sqn could even begin flying, and even then only three or four SBDs could be

made operational on average. Consequently, four more 'dash threes' were obtained, with a further nine SBD-4s on hand by September.

The first 18 Dauntlesses received serial numbers in the NZ200 range, but eventually RNZAF SBDs were allotted the NZ5000 series. The SBD-3s therefore had two serial numbers each, in addition to their US Navy 'BuAer' identification!

Despite the problems, No 25 Sqn quickly got on with its transition programme. Dauntless conversion took six hours dual instruction and sixteen solo, including ten hours on instruments. Owing to the SBD's poor forward visibility from the rear cockpit, two Harvards were obtained to facilitate instrument flight training.

Meanwhile, the squadron had adopted its crest and motto. The badge depicted a Caspian Tern diving with a bomb in its claws, and the Moari motto *kia kaha* was interpreted as 'constant endeavour'.

No 25 Sqn trained in three types of attacks – a 75-degree dive, a 45-degree glide and masthead attacks intended against enemy submarines, with a 50-ft pullout. By the time the squadron was ready to deploy to combat, pilots had logged 100 to 200 hours in type, and wireless operator air gunners (WAOGs) 60 to 120. Before departure, MacLean led 18 Dauntlesses in formation over Auckland on 6 January 1944, which was reportedly the most aircraft yet seen over the capitol.

During an interim period at Pallikulo, on Espiritu Santo, No 25 Sqn

The only dive bomber unit in the RNZAF was No 25 Sqn, formed by Sqn Ldr T J MacLean de Lange at Seagrove in July 1943. Originally issued with nine SBD-3s provided by the US Marine Corps' Air Group 14, the 'loaner' Dauntlesses were augmented when 13 additional SBD-3s and -4s arrived for operational training. This aircraft, bearing the side number 5, was photographed during a familiarisation flight over New Zealand (*René Francillon*)

Although the Dauntless was an easy aircraft to fly, accidents were inevitable. At the end of operational training the New Zealanders averaged nearly 200 hours 'in type', with air gunners between 60 and 120 hours. This SBD-4, NZ5024, groundlooped on landing (note the damage to the port wingtip) and nosed up in soft earth. The small, hard tailwheel normally retained by carrier-based aircraft is clearly visible in this view (*René Francillon*)

drew 18 SBD-4s from the Marine Corps and flew practise missions during February. These aircraft were in no better condition than those left in New Zealand, but later that month new SBD-5s were issued. Eventually the squadron operated 24 to maintain a nominal roster of 18 Dauntlesses.

On 22 March No 25 Sqn began staging north to Piva airfield on Bougainville, via Henderson Field, Guadalcanal. Sqn Ldr de Lange's 22 crews were committed to action almost immediately, tasked with 12 sorties by Solomons Strike Command on typical days from an average strength of 15 aircraft.

No 25 Sqn entered combat in March 1944, flying 23 SBD-5s from Bougainville. Over the next two months the Kiwis flew strikes against Rabaul, New Britain, in company with US Marine and other Allied units. Here, NZ5056 taxies along Piva's pierced-steel matting with a 500-lb bomb on the centreline rack and a 100-pounder beneath each wing. Although no combat losses occurred during the squadron's two months at Bougainville, six aircraft, three pilots and two gunners were lost to operational causes (*René Francillon*)

Missions to Rabaul concentrated on two areas – various targets bordering Simpson, and Vunakanau airfield, about ten miles south of Rabaul town. A round trip mission took 3.5 to 4.0 hours, and frequently No 25 Sqn flew as part of a 60- to 80-aircraft strike in company with American and other RNZAF aircraft. A typical mission involved 48 Dauntlesses and 24 Avengers, plus fighter escorts.

In eight weeks of operations No 25 Sqn's aircrews averaged about 30 strike missions with no combat losses. However, in all the squadron lost six Dauntlesses, three pilots and two WOAGs in various accidents. On 20 May 1944 the unit rotated southward, returning its colourfully-marked aircraft to the Marine facility in the Russell Islands. MacLean's personnel then proceeded home in a Dakota.

A second Dauntless unit, No 26 Sqn, had been considered but was never formed because RNZAF headquarters determined that fighters such as Kittyhawks and Corsairs could perform as well at ground attack. The SBDs left in storage in New Zealand remained at Hobsonville airfield until sold for scrap in November 1947.

Thirty years after No 25 Sqn made its record, RNZAF historian Sqn Ldr Cliff Jenks summarised the Dauntless as 'a successful failure'. The 69 SBDs that wore RNZAF cockades were judged to have arrived too late to make a lasting impression, but their aircrews became full partners with the US Marine Corps in the reduction of the greatest Japanese bastion in the Southwest Pacific.

THE FRENCH CONNECTION

France was unique among the combatants of World War 2 in that her airmen both fought SBDs and flew them as well. During Operation *Torch* (the Allied invasion of Vichy-controlled Morocco in November 1942), US Navy squadrons bombed and strafed French naval and military targets. However, two years later Free French aircrews flew SBDs against German opponents in Europe.

Free French squadrons received between 40 and 50 A-24Bs in 1943, with initial training conducted in Morocco and Algeria. *Groupe de Combat* I/17 'Picardie' flew a variety of second-line Allied aircraft, with one *escadrille* assigned A-24s for coastal patrol.

Free French squadrons received 40 to 50 A-24Bs in Morocco and Algeria during 1943. These weather-beaten aircraft may belong to *Groupe de Combat* I/17's *escadrille* that conducted coastal patrols during that period. Previous USAAF tail numbers have been painted over in favour of the vertical rudder stripes on the second and third aircraft, numbers 23 and 27 (*René Francillon*)

The most combat-experienced of the French Banshee units was GC I/18 *Vendee*, flying A-24Bs in support of Allied forces in the South of France during 1944. However, as the war progressed northward, the Banshees found both coastal and inland targets around Lorient and Bordeaux. This aircraft, USAAF s/n 42-54541, bears both the French cockade and the red Cross of Lorraine on a white background, while retaining the standard American olive-drab over grey paint scheme (*René Francillon*)

In early 1944 a new group was established with the intent of supplying French resistance units by air. *Groupe de Combat* I/18 'Vendee' was designated a fighter-bomber organisation with a heavy influx of experienced A-24 crews from Syria and Morocco. With the Anglo-American invasion of Southern France in August, Commandant Lapios' unit flew to recently liberated Toulouse.

As the German defenders retreated, 'Vendee' aviators flew repeated missions in early September, keeping the pressure on the enemy. However, the Germany army's scientifically-designed flak system could be murderous – three A-24s were shot down in two days, whilst most of the survivors were damaged.

As Allied forces drove farther into France, GC I/18 proved its value repeatedly. Dive-bombing missions were assigned to the group along the Atlantic coast, helping reduce German strongholds and isolating port cities such as Lorient and Bordeaux. The opportunity also arose for anti-shipping missions as Nazi-controlled vessels attempted to keep supplies flowing into bypassed ports.

By the end of the war in Europe in May 1945, the 25 surviving A-24s were returned to Morocco, where they were used as trainers. According to French historian J Cuny, the last Banshees were grounded in 1953.

Following Operation *Anvil-Dragoon* in the Riviera, French naval aviation (the *Aeronautique Navale*) also received SBD-5s. Formed and trained in Morocco in late 1944, two squadrons, or *flotilles*, were built around aircrews who had previously flown Martin 167s and Vought 156s – the latter being export models of the SB2U scout bomber.

Flotilles 3FB and 4FB were each assigned 16 Dauntlesses under the administrative control of *Groupe Aeronavale No 2*. Flying from Cognac, they logged their first combat missions on 9 December 1944. Like their air force counterparts, the naval aviators found German 20 mm and 37 mm flak a menace, as four of the five combat losses were attributable to anti-aircraft fire. The other loss was caused by premature ordnance detonation.

However, the Dauntless proved itself in the European Theatre when GAN 2 averaged 72 sorties a day during one week in April 1945 – an average of three missions per aircraft per day.

After the war, *Aeronautique Navale* crews finally were able to put their naval aircraft to 'proper' use – at sea. *Flotilles* 3F and 4F operated from the former HMS *Biter* as *Dixmunde* and HMS *Colossus* as *Arromanches* until at least 1949.

French Air Force A-24s were employed after the war in operational
training both in France and Morocco. Additionally, some Banshees were
flown by the Moroccan desert police, possibly as late as 1953.

An additional foreign user of the Banshee was Mexico, one *esquadra* of
the *Fuerza Aerea Mexicana* training on 26 A-24s before converting to P-
47Ds for combat with the USAAF's Fifth Air Force in the Philippines.
The Douglases later flew localised anti-submarine patrols over the Gulf of
Mexico from 1944, but by then the U-boats' 'second happy time' had
long ended in American waters.

Although only committed to foreign service in small numbers, the
SBD/A-24 series dramatically expanded the type's global role – from the
Pacific and Atlantic to the Mediterranean and continental Europe itself,
the dive-bombers from Tulsa and El Segundo made themselves felt
against the forces of Germany as well as Japan.

PERSPECTIVE

T he Dauntless served far beyond its intended lifespan, flying combat missions in the Pacific, European and Mediterranean theatres of operations with six air arms – the US Navy, Marine Corps and Army, the French Air Force and Navy, and the Royal New Zealand Air Force. And, despite a lack of combat opportunity, the Mexican Air Force became the seventh service to fly the type during World War 2.

To meet the demands of so many 'clients', production of the SBD and A-24 far exceeded Douglas or Navy plans at the time of Pearl Harbor. From 332 in all of 1941, El Segundo built 864 Dauntlesses in 1942 and more than 3000 in 1943, not to mention the Tulsa, Oklahoma, plant which manufactured Banshees. The peak month was May 1943 when 419 SBD-5s and A-24Bs were accepted by the BuAer representatives at El Segundo.

Throughout the critical 12 months after the Japanese attack on Pearl Harbor, the SBD was both numerically and operationally the most important American carrier aircraft. In the prewar air group composition, including both bombing and scouting squadrons, SBDs represented half of the nominal 72 aircraft aboard a typical fleet carrier.

The SBD's importance to victory in the Pacific is best stated in one statistic – no other American aircraft participated in every carrier battle from Coral Sea in May 1942 through to the Philippine Sea in June 1944. Midway, of course, remains the pinnacle of Dauntless attainment, sinking no fewer than four Japanese carriers in one day, and thereby reversing the course of the Pacific War. Never was the US Navy's reliance upon dive-bombing – and its proficiency in that esoteric martial art – better illustrated.

Even when fighting squadrons were raised to 27 and then 36 Wildcats in the second half of 1942, Dauntlesses retained their significance as the Navy's most effective strike aircraft throughout the long Guadalcanal campaign.

Certainly Marine Corps SBDs dominated the offensive potential of American aircraft at Henderson Field on Guadalcanal itself. Although ably assisted by small numbers of Grumman TBF Avengers, Dauntlesses were primarily responsible for maintaining the tenuous lifeline in the constant battle for control of the waters in the southern Solomons. Army Air Force types as diverse as Bell P-39 Airaco-

As if fading into history, an *Enterprise* SBD-5 banks away, ordnance expended, in this early 1944 photo. Throughout the war, CV 6 aircrews consistently sustained heavier losses than any other carrier – 27 pilots and 29 radioman-gunners, these totals representing nearly half of *all* carrier-based SBD aircrew fatalities

A midwar publicity photo posed for Navy recruiters to draw qualified youngsters into the combat aircrewman programme. Complete with a stencilled Japanese flag (extreme right), this picture evokes the glamour associated with aircrew status, but behind most frontline 'airdales' was a year or more of training in communications, electronics, gunnery and squadron work-ups before reaching the combat zone

bras and Boeing B-17 Flying Fortresses provided occasional assistance, but neither type was well suited to the anti-shipping role. Furthermore, the American torpedo scandal of 1942 significantly reduced the TBF's contribution to 'derailing' the 'Tokyo Express' which supplied Japanese Army forces on Guadalcanal.

One of the greatest ironies of the SBD's career is the prospect that America could have lost Guadalcanal if the SB2C Helldiver had become operational in 1941 or early 1942. By retaining the 'obsolescent' Dauntless instead of the newer Curtiss aircraft, the 'Cactus Air Force' was provided with a reliable, easily maintained, aircraft in an environment not the least conducive to sophistication. Always a high maintenance aeroplane, the SB2C's complex hydraulics and other systems were difficult enough aboard well-equipped fleet carriers. But in Henderson Field's crude, dusty atmosphere, with chronic shortages of fuel, spare parts and tools, it is unlikely the Helldiver could have provided the sortie rates which even the SBD was hard pressed to maintain.

In the Central Pacific, land-based SBDs hauled the majority of bomb tonnage against bypassed enemy islands until late 1944. Increasing numbers of F4U Corsairs and, eventually, SB2C Helldivers, eventually assumed greater portions of the responsibility in the Marshall Islands, but the Dauntless was never fully supplanted in that role.

Similarly, Marine SBDs were instrumental in the protracted effort to recapture the Philippines. Unprecedented in American military history was the SBD's mission in protecting the flank of the First Cavalry Division during its drive on Manila. Solely relying upon dive-bombers to keep enemy forces off his exposed manoeuvre elements, the division commander was lavish in his praise of the flying 'Leathernecks'. It was an ironic reversal in which the Marines, who influenced Luftwaffe interest in the dive-bomber during the 1930s, duplicated the role of the Junkers Ju 87 Stuka in guarding the flanks of Wehrmacht advances, first in Poland and later in the USSR.

Aviators' recollections of the aeroplane are uniformly favourable. Here are the thoughts of just a few notable SBD pilots;

Richard H Best, CO VB-6, *Enterprise*
'Aside from a general affection that a service pilot may have for a plane that he has flown for some time, he is not inclined to have any outstanding recollections unless it was some cranky characteristics or heart-stopping moments. The plane from which the SBD was mocked up was the Northrop BT-1. In its early form it had a very bad wingroot stall characteristic which left you out of control while the ailerons still felt solid.

There was vastly more to putting a dive-bomber over its target than pilot and aircrew training. This photo, possibly from *Lexington* in the summer of 1943, demonstrates the intricate teamwork required of plane directors, handlers and (in the foreground) flight deck officers to co-ordinate the 'organised chaos' inherent to aircraft carrier operations. The constant danger posed by propellers was compounded by the inability of deckcrewmen to communicate vocally owing to engine noise

Leading edge slots and a 3-degree twist on the wing fixed that, and therefore fixed the SBD.

'Aside from that, my outstanding recollection of the accessories to the plane concern the armoured seat that was put in about the time the war started. It was so heavy that the bungee cord could not ordinarily handle it. When you released the lever to lower it, you descended with a jolt – to raise it again took the leg muscles of a weight lifter.

'The rear seat body armour attached to the scarff ring during the first month or so of the war frightened the gunners. With bulky flying clothes and all the parachute straps around the body, there was a good chance that if the pilot got shaky and went out in a hurry, the rear seat man would go down with the plane. When I realised that my rear seat man had been getting up-tight for a week or two and questioned him, I first learned about this concern. I assured him that I would never leave the plane until after he was gone, and I never saw signs of his being upset again.

'The other thing that I first noticed was the Wright engine. It sounded great in flight but on the ground it loped very disconcertingly. I spent all my time up until then in Pratt & Whitneys, which purred like kittens. It's a psychological drawback, but it's the only thing I had against the plane.'

Harold L Buell, VS-5, *Yorktown*, and VB-10, *Enterprise*

'The standard load on either a VB or VS SBD leaving the "Big E" or *Yorktown* for a search or anti-submarine patrol in 1942 was a 500-lb general purpose bomb. Standard loading for all attacks by VS-5 aircraft at Tulagi-Coral Sea, and in support of the Guadalcanal landings and sea battles, was a 1000-lb bomb, both from *Yorktown* and *Enterprise*. However, as Flight 300 flying from Henderson Field in the "Cactus Air Force", we carried, for the most part, 500-pounders – that was all we had, and the original field surface, before Marston matting was laid, was too short and rough for an SBD to get airborne with more than a 500. After lengthening the field and matting the surface, I'm sure that 1000-pounders were used.

'As for spotting of VS or VB aircraft on the flight deck, as I remember it was mostly luck as to who went first – we stressed more the grouping of aircraft so that we could be launched in sequence to aid squadron and division rendezvous, especially if it was a pre-dawn launch.

'I do not remember ever having a 500-lb bomb load based solely upon the amount of deck run available. Where the trouble came was when a CV would not provide enough knots to give adequate relative wind down the deck for a safe take-off regardless of loading. Of course, by mid-1943 we had a wider selection of bombs and loads in the SB2Cs, with semi-armour-piercing, napalm and even some 2000-pounders.

'Unlike some dive-bomber pilots, I do not condemn the Helldiver – I got some fine hits with it, and it brought many a pilot home with heavy battle damage. I do stress the point that the SB2C Helldiver was a much harder aircraft to fly as a weapon than the SBD, and not as forgiving of mistakes, thus it was a greater nemesis to the young, inexperienced "nugget" ensigns we were getting as both new squadron pilots and replacements.'

Maxwell F Leslie, CO VB-3, *Saratoga* and *Yorktown*

'There were many types of military planes used during World War 2 with any of them being recalled as the most effective against the enemy, but in my opinion there isn't a doubt that the SBD should be near the top of the list. I can't think of a single feature which could have made it more qualified for its designed mission.

'The horsepower was sufficient to permit us to cruise at 165 knots and thus keep up with the F4Fs which were our protective fighters. The later models had leakproof gasoline tanks which probably saved the life of more than one pilot. Both the pilot and rear gunner had bulletproof back protection.

'The dive flaps gave the plane the steadiest dive of any of the several dive-bombers I flew. Electric bomb releases in place of the old manual ones were a big improvement because of the split-second timing required to drop a bomb. The only slight defect was the fact that the original telescope sight usually fogged over and destroyed some of the accuracy desired. Changes in atmospheric conditions caused this phenomenon, and it was a tough one to combat. It required pilots to use the alternate open air sight, and it wasn't as accurate as the telescope (until reflector sights became available in the SBD-5).'

Bruce Prosser, VMSB-232, Guadalcanal

'One item frequently overlooked is that originally the SBDs were high performance planes. In fact, a stripped-down version could hold its own very creditably with the fighters of that period. However, with the installation of armour plate, external bomb and rocket rails and extensive electronic gear, the old girl was severely penalised in performance.

'Generally speaking, the plane was rugged, stable, dependable, versatile and could effectively deliver a wide variety of dissimilar ordnance. The particular dive flap arrangement made the SBD one of the most stable, heavy ordnance delivery platforms that I have ever used. Also, the plane's delivery speed could be adjusted to the pilot's advantage. I used to like to push over and then pop those flaps in the dive.

'The old girl had one particular characteristic – in a tight vertical left-hand turn she stopped flying without warning and her nose dropped quickly and significantly. I allowed plenty of altitude for this manoeuvre. Turning vertically to the right, the action was slower and not as pronounced.'

In summary, the Dauntless was the right aeroplane for the war it had to fight. It was a rugged, simple aircraft with no serious vices. Easily maintained, it afforded high in-commission rates wherever adequate facilities were available. Although nowhere as fast as its contemporaries, it had sufficient range and payload which, coupled with precision bombing, made it the most effective naval strike aircraft of World War 2.

Speed brakes deployed, an SBD pushes over for a practise dive. At terminal velocity of some 240 mph, the Dauntless plunged from 15,000 ft to release altitude in 30 to 35 seconds, with a normal release altitude of between 1500 and 2000 ft. In that time a warship could cover nearly 200 yards, requiring smooth, constant tracking in order to place the bomb accurately (NP)

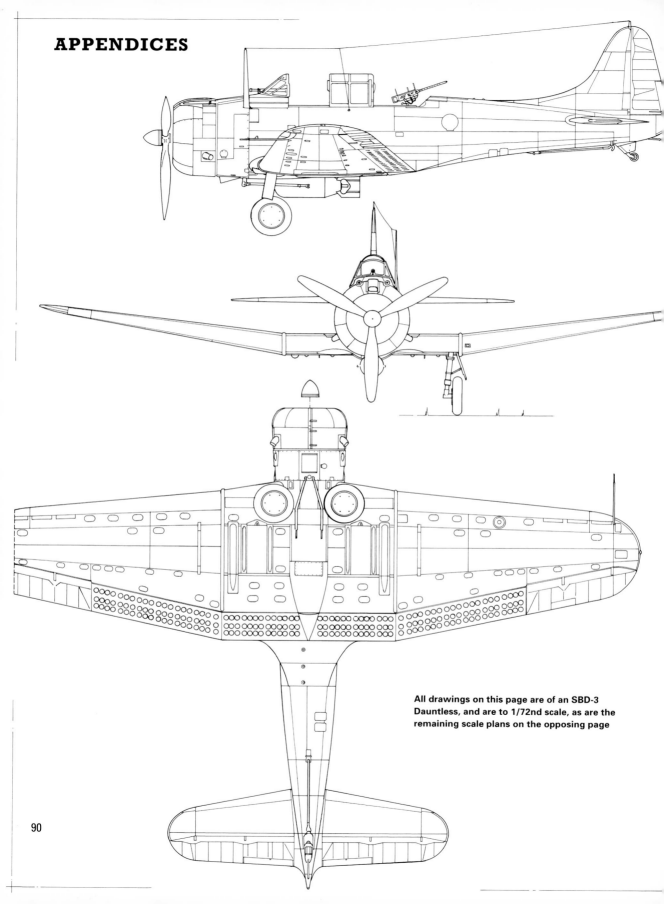

APPENDICES

All drawings on this page are of an SBD-3
Dauntless, and are to 1/72nd scale, as are the
remaining scale plans on the opposing page

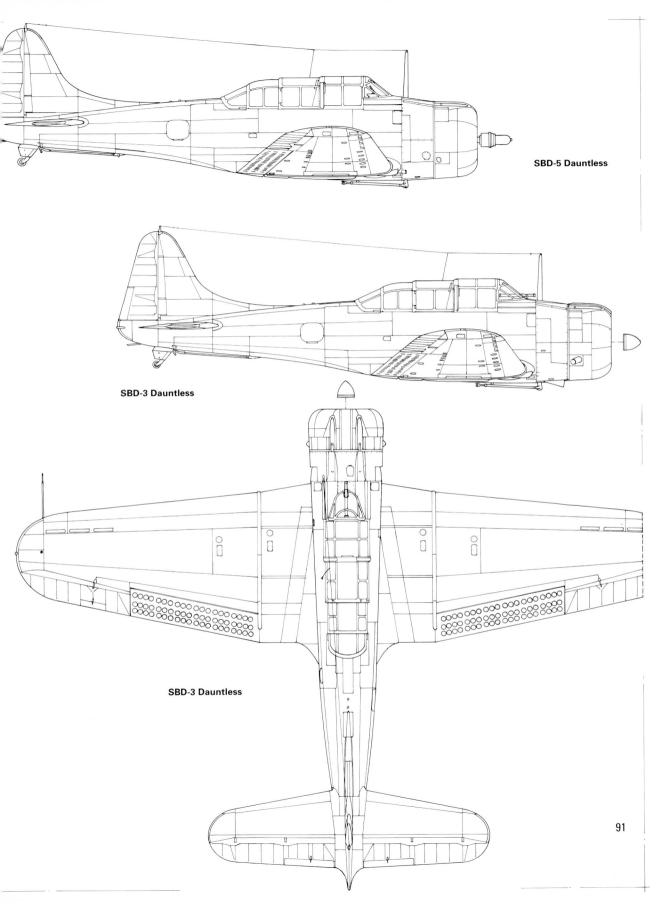

SBD-5 Dauntless

SBD-3 Dauntless

SBD-3 Dauntless

91

COLOUR PLATES

1

SBD-3 BuNo 03213 White 0, flown by Cdr Harry D Felt and Chief Radioman Cletus A Snyder, USS *Saratoga* (CV 3), August 1942

Felt was one of the early SBD pilots, having led Bombing Two when the squadron received SBD-2s in 1940. By the summer of 1942 he was commander of Saratoga's air group, flying 'Queen Bee' BuNo 03213. Felt may have been the first CAG to fly an aircraft numbered '0'. In this aircraft he led the successful attack against IJNS *Ryujo* on 24 August, resulting in her sinking. The rising sun flag painted ahead of the cockpit signified the bomb hit Felt claimed on the enemy ship. Mission markers and 'kill' emblems were rare on SBDs, the main exception for the former seeming to have been some squadrons assigned to the Fourth Marine Air Wing in the Central Pacific during 1944-45. Squadron emblems such as the VMSB-231 ace of spades were also more common in such areas than aboard ships. Rising sun 'victory flags' were exceptional on SBDs at any time. Erroneous profiles published in the past 30 years display 'meatballs' on some scout-bombers, especially the Scouting Two aircraft of Lt(jg) Leppla and Radioman Liska. However, at least two carriers briefly enjoyed the practise of victory flags. Aside from Felt's 'Queen Bee', *Wasp*'s two Dauntless squadrons flaunted their success over Japanese aircraft at the start of the Guadalcanal campaign, as SBDs shot down seven enemy aircraft before the fighters scored at all. The aircraft was subsequently damaged in a carrier landing and jettisoned several months after Cdr Felt had left CV 3.

2

SBD-3 BuNo 4531 White S-11, flown by Cdr William B Ault and Radioman 1st Class William T Butler, USS *Lexington* (CV 2), 8 May 1942.

Though Ault had an assigned 'CAG bird', he flew this Scouting Two aircraft during the 8 May attack on *Shokaku* in the Coral Sea battle. Intercepted by defending A6M2 Zeros, Ault's SBD was damaged and apparently he and his gunner were wounded. He made a radio call that his formation had obtained bomb hits on the enemy carrier, then disappeared into worsening weather. Contrary to drawings published over the past several decades, evidently no *Lexington* aircraft displayed squadron insignia, nor bore the full legend such as 2-S-11. The S-11 was applied in white by VS-2, whilst Bombing Two used black. Tactical markings were simplified in the weeks after Pearl Harbor, the full legend 2-S-11, for example, being shortened by deleting the first digit, which identified the ship as well as the squadron. White prewar numbers largely disappeared in favour of black figures.

3

SBD-3 BuNo 4537 White S-8 of Scouting Two, flown by Lt(jg) William E Hall and Seaman 1st Class John A Moore, USS *Lexington* (CV 2), 8 May 1942

Hall was awarded the Medal of Honor for his 8 May action

in this aircraft while defending *Lexington* from Japanese carrier attack. Assigned to the low-level anti-torpedo aircraft patrol, Hall was seriously wounded in one foot but remained in the fight and shot down at least one Nakajima B5N attacking his ship. His Dauntless was so badly shot up that it was jettisoned overboard soon after landing back aboard the doomed *Lexington*. Like S-11, this aircraft had white numbers identifying it as a scout, but no number was displayed on the cowling – the individual number was probably repeated on the leading edge of each wing. This SBD shows typical early-war markings as worn by most carrier-based aircraft in the Pacific until Midway. The combat evolution of carrier aircraft schemes had began in early 1942, by which time some air groups had already begun painting airframe upper surfaces blue-grey for less contrast over water. To enhance recognition of 'friendlies', on 5 January the Navy authorised the painting of 13 red and white horizontal rudder stripes, while wing stars were enlarged to full chord width, overlapping the ailerons. Photographic evidence indicates a great deal of non-conformity over the ensuing four months, some aircraft having both large- and small-diameter stars on wings and/or fuselage, and a few with none of the latter.

4

SBD-3 Black B-1 of Bombing Three, flown by Lt Cdr Maxwell F Leslie and ARM1/c W E Gallagher, USS *Yorktown* (CV 5), 4 June 1942

Leslie led VB-3's attack on IJNS *Soryu* during the morning strike at the Battle of Midway. Despite having lost his 1000-lb bomb en route to the target (as did three other VB-3 pilots), he was the first to dive on the Japanese carrier, helping suppress anti-aircraft fire with his forward-firing .50 calibre guns. *Soryu* was sunk in this attack, and although Leslie returned safely to the US task force, he ran out of fuel while awaiting conclusion of the Japanese retaliatory strike from *Hiryu*. He landed safely alongside the light cruiser *Astoria* and was rescued with Gallagher. Note how this aircraft has the post-15 May 1942 markings that saw the striped rudder and 'meatball' in the white star deleted in order to avoid confusion with Japanese markings. By Midway and Guadalcanal, most SBDs typically bore the blue-grey over light grey scheme with plain white stars in six positions. Unit markings continued in black.

5

SBD-3 Black B-46 of Bombing Three, flown by Lt(jg) Robert M Elder and Radioman 2nd Class LA Till, USS *Saratoga* (CV 3), 24 August 1942

During the Eastern Solomons battle, Elder participated in a seven-aircraft strike against a reported enemy carrier force late that afternoon. While five Avengers attacked another formation, Elder led his wingman, Ens R T Gordon, against the seaplane tender *Chitose* and inflicted heavy damage that nearly sank the ship. Elder's radioman-gunner, L A Till, also flew with him at Midway. Note the the LSO stripe across the vertical stabiliser, this marking dating from at least 1940. The visual aid for landing signal officers usually comprised just one diagonal line (although two were occasionally used), its application helping to indicate to the LSO whether the pilot had adopted the proper nose-up attitude for his approach to the deck. Most LSO stripes were white, although prior to Pearl Harbor red had also been used.

6

SBD-5 Black S-1 of VMS-3, flown by Maj Christian C Lee, US Virgin Islands, May 1944

The only Marine Corps squadron to fly SBDs in the Caribbean was Scouting Three, which had a mixed complement including Dauntlesses and OS2U Kingfishers. Mainly engaged in anti-submarine patrol work, the squadron was disbanded when the potential U-boat threat disappeared. The distinctive Atlantic colour scheme of insignia white and blue-grey was among the most attractive of the era. Most of the squadron's SBDs had names painted in black script immediately behind the cowling. VMS-3 was disestablished at St Thomas, Virgin Islands, in May 1944.

7

SBD-3 BuNo 2132 Black 16 of Bombing Five, flown by Ens Davis E Chaffee and Seaman 1st Class John A Kasselman, USS *Yorktown* (CV 5), 8 May 1942.

On 8 May, the second day of the Battle of the Coral Sea, Yorktown Air Group combined with *Lexington* squadrons to attack the Japanese carriers covering the Port Moresby invasion force. The American squadrons became dispersed in heavy clouds and low ceilings which interfered with the type of co-ordinated attack that had sunk IJNS *Shoho* the day before. However, Bombing five dived on IJNS *Shokaku* and inflicted damage for the loss of two crews. 5-B-16 was lost with Ens Chaffee and Seaman Kasselman, while Lt J J Powers and Radioman E C Hill were also killed.

8

SBD-3 BuNo 4690 Black S-10 of Scouting Five, flown by Lt(jg) Stanley W Vejtasa and Radioman 3rd Class Frank B Wood, USS *Yorktown* (CV 5), 8 May 1942.

Following the US task force's strike against *Shokaku* and *Zuikaku* on 8 May, *Lexington* and *Yorktown* were attacked by squadrons from both Japanese carriers. Among eight VS-5 crews assigned to a low-level anti-torpedo aircraft patrol was Lt(jg) 'Swede' Vejtasa and his gunner, Radioman Frank Wood. In the ensuing wavetop melee, A6M2 Zeros shot down four scouts with all crews lost. Vejtasa flew his SBD aggressively, offering only deflection shots to the fighters, and was credited with three destroyed – only one A6M actually ditched with battle damage. Vejtasa was awarded the Navy Cross and soon joined VF-10, where he won a second award for his interception of Japanese torpedo bombers at Santa Cruz in October 1942 (see *Osprey Aircraft of the Aces 3 - Wildcat Aces of World War 2* also by Barrett Tillman for further details).

9

SBD-3 Black 17 of Scouting Five, flown by Ens Leif Larsen and Radioman John F Gardner, USS *Yorktown* (CV 5), June 1942

For the brief Midway deployment, Bombing Five was redesignated Scouting Five to avoid confusion with Bombing Three, which replaced VS-5 in Yorktown Air Group. The fuselage number was repeated in black on the leading edge of the wings just inboard of the fairing over the wing stub and outer panel. No LSO stripes were carried. This aircraft was unusual in that the undersurface medium grey colour was extended upwards along the front of the engine cowling to the air scoop.

10

SBD-3 BuNo 4687 Black B-1 of Bombing Six, flown by Lt Richard H Best and Chief Radioman James F Murray, USS *Enterprise* (CV 6), 4 June 1942

As the commanding officer of VB-6, Best flew this aircraft on two missions during the Battle of Midway. In the first sortie he led his squadron the attacks on IJNS *Akagi* and *Kaga*, whilst during the second (flown late that afternoon) he helped sink IJNS *Hiryu*. Later that day Best was sidelined with lung problems derived from inhaling caustic soda generated in a faulty oxygen bottle. It led to his premature retirement from active duty, but on his last day of flying he had helped sink two enemy aircraft carriers!

11

SBD-3 Black B-18 of Bombing Six, flown by Ensign Robert C Shaw and AO2/c Harold L Jones, USS *Enterprise*, 8 August 1942

Shaw and Jones were part of a formation of eight VB-6 and VS-5 aircraft designated as Flight 319 on *Enterprise's* operations schedule. While orbiting near Tulagi that morning, waiting for a target to be assigned, the SBDs were attacked by two A6M2 Zeros from Rabaul, New Britain. The lead fighter was flown by Petty Officer Saburo Sakai, who sustained grievous injuries from the return fire of two or more scout-bombers. Though blinded in one eye, Sakai managed to fly more than 500 miles back to Rabaul.

12

Douglas SBD-5 White 19 of VB-9, USS *Essex* (CV 9), early 1944

Simple but prominent tail numbers marked the aircraft of Bombing Squadron Nine, part of Air Group Nine aboard *Essex* for nearly a year beginning in March 1943. Combat actions during this period spanned the Wake Island strike of October 1943 to the first Truk attack in February 1944. The fuselage star and bars shows evidence of overpainting the original red outline, which was replaced with a full insignia blue surround.

13

SBD-3 Black S4 of Scouting Six, USS *Enterprise*, February 1942

During the early months of 1942, American carrier aircraft bore a hodge-podge of markings, especially where national insignia were concerned. This Dauntless of Scouting

Squadron Six was rare even by the standards of that hectic period due to its lack of fuselage stars. 'Sail Four' was briefly marked like this almost certainly during the February Wake Island strike. Also unusual was the presentation of the numeral 4, without the 'tail' of the cross stroke extending beyond the vertical line. Other VS-6 aircraft at the same time displayed both the large and small fuselage star, with the side number either forward or aft of the emblem.

14

SBD-3 BuNo 06492 Black S-13 of Scouting 10, flown by Lt Stockton B Strong and Radioman 1st Class Clarence H Garlow, USS *Enterprise*, 26 October 1942

In one of *the* classic Dauntless missions of the war, Strong successfully attacked the Japanese carrier *Zuiho* during the Battle of Santa Cruz. Scouting an adjacent sector, he was informed of a contact report and navigated to the enemy's position some 150 miles away. Strong and his wingman, Ens Charles Irvin, both claimed hits that put the light carrier out of the battle. In the low-level pursuit following the attack, Garlow claimed a Zero shot down. Strong later commanded VB-10, informing a new pilot, 'I'm going to make you the second best bomber in the Pacific!' He finished the war as an F4U squadron commander aboard USS *Shangri-La* (CV 38).

15

SBD-3 White B16 of Bombing 11, flown by Lt(jg) Edwin Wilson and Radioman 2nd Class Harry Jespersen, Guadalcanal, summer 1943

VB-11 was land-based throughout the Solomons campaign, although it had originally been sent to the Pacific as the intended replacement unit for the original *Hornet* (CV 8), sunk at Santa Cruz in October 1942. Flying from Henderson Field between April and July 1943, Wilson and Jespersen used this aircraft on many of their missions. The 16 was repeated on the upper surface of the wing, and the squadron emblem was carried on both sides of the fuselage – a white shield with the black winged Pegasus, as previously used by *Lexington's* Bombing Two. Nearly all carrier squadrons had displayed unit emblems prior to late 1941: Scouting Two's indian chief; Bombing Three's leaping panther; Bombing Five's winged devil; Bombing Six's charging ram. However, such insignia were seldom displayed in combat, partly as a security measure and partly owing to frequent reassignment of scarce aircraft during the frantic year after Pearl Harbor. Bombing Eleven was one of the first Navy units to revive the tradition, adopting VB-2's Bellerophon, while VMSB-231 followed suit by retaining its classic Ace of Spades marking. The original CO of VB-11 was Lt Cdr Weldon Hamilton, who took four of his former VB-2 pilots to his new command – hence the Bombing Two emblem.

16

SBD-5 White 39 of Bombing Sixteen, flown by Lt Cook Cleland and Radioman 2nd Class William J Hisler, USS *Lexington* (CV 16), June 1944

Cook Cleland became best known for his victories in the postwar Thompson Trophy races in modified F2G

Corsairs. However, his combat service in VB-16 included two aerial victories over enemy aircraft, Cleland downing a 'Sonia' ground attack aircraft near Hollandia, in New Guinea, on 21 April 1944, and his gunner, Radioman W J Hisler, claiming a Zeke over the Japanese Mobile Fleet on 20 June, with a second fighter damaged. At the completion of the latter mission, most VB-16 aircraft had insufficient fuel for another pass at the flight deck upon returning to *Lexington*.

17

SBD-5 White 17 of Composite Squadron 29, USS *Santee* (CVE 29), North Atlantic, 1943

These mid-war markings were unusual in that the full designation was applied between the cockpits with the black 29C, followed by a larger white individual aircraft number. The overall colour scheme was sea grey upper and medium grey under surfaces, with national insignia applied in six positions on most of the squadron's aeroplanes, but sometimes only in four places (upper port and lower starboard wings plus both sides of the fuselage).

18

SBD-3 Black 41-S-7 of Scouting 41, USS *Ranger* (CV 4), November 1942

The distinctive yellow ring around the national insignia identified Allied aircraft involved in Operation *Torch* – the invasion of French Morocco in November 1942. SBDs from *Ranger* and other escort carriers provided support for US Army troops at three landing beaches, as well as attacking Vichy French warships both in Casablanca Harbour and offshore.

19

SBD-5 Black 108 of VS-51, Tutuila, Samoa, May 1944

By mid 1944 the majority of deployed Navy SBD squadrons were inshore scouting units based in rear areas. Their main purpose was anti-submarine patrol, although that threat was much diminished by then. This VS-51 aircraft bears the standard tricolour scheme with simple unit markings in the form of three-digit numeral below the gunner's cockpit. The tricolour scheme first appeared on Dauntlesses late on in the SBD-4's production run, the colours being from top to bottom, matte dark blue, medium blue and insignia white undersurfaces, with shading or 'feathering' to blend each demarcation line. The earliest tricolour SBDs kept the 1942 national insignia, but in mid 1943 white horizontal bars were added to smaller-diameter stars in four positions. A narrow red border surrounded the emblem from June to September that year. Note that the usual hard rubber tailwheel for carrier use has been replaced on this aircraft by the larger pneumatic type, which was more suited to land operations.

20

SBD-3 BuNo 03315 Black 16 of Scouting 71, USS *Wasp* (CV 7), August 1942

On 25 August this SBD was flown by two pilots to shoot down three Japanese aircraft. On the morning search Lt(jg) Chester V Zalewski splashed two Aichi E13A 'Jake' floatplanes from the cruisers *Atago* and *Haguro*, whilst that afternoon Lt Morris R Doughty led his division against a Kawanishi H8K 'Emily', which was shot down – the SBDs had been on an anti-shipping strike at the time. Although all four Dauntlesses were involved in the latter action, Doughty was credited with the kill. Three documented victory flags on one SBD undoubtedly stood as a record!

21

SBD-5 White 101 of VB-98, Munda, New Georgia, March 1944

Among the land-based US Navy squadrons operating against Rabaul, New Britain, was VB-98. Largely flying from Munda in that period, the squadron was typical of many AirSols units in that it did not belong to a parent air group. Following the reduction of Rabaul, the need for many such squadrons quickly lapsed, and VB-98 was disestablished that summer. Note the unusual size and location of the fuselage 'star and bar', which has been placed farther forward than normal.

22

SBD-4/5 White 119 *PUSH PUSH* of VMSB-144, flown by Maj Frank E Hollar, Solomon Islands, November 1943

Based at Munda in the New Georgia group, VMSB-144 supported the landings at Empress Augusta Bay on Bougainville. The aircraft name *PUSH PUSH* was unusual even by Marine Corps standards, both in respect to its existence and prominent size. Hollar led the squadron from April to late November 1943, after which -144 returned to the USA to be redesignated a torpedo bombing squadron with Avengers.

23

SBD-1 White 232-MB-2 of VMSB-232, MCAS Ewa, Territory of Hawaii, 7 December 1941

Wearing standard prewar overall light grey, this Marine Corps Dauntless survived the Japanese surprise attack on the 'day of infamy'. Largely destroyed on the ground, VMSB-232 slowly rebuilt over the next several months until deployed to Guadalcanal in August 1942. Under Maj Richard C Mangrum, -232 was the first bombing squadron of what became famous as 'The Cactus Air Force'.

24

SBD-5 White 1 of VMSB-231 flown by Maj Elmer Glidden, and M/Sgt James Boyle, Marshall Islands, 1944

The 'Ace of Spades' squadron was one of the oldest in the Marine Corps, and Maj Glidden was the service's leading dive-bomber pilot. Having flown SBD-2s at Midway and -3s at Guadalcanal, he logged 77 more combat dives in the Marshalls for a wartime total of 104. Glidden flew this Dauntless in the Marshalls, with his missions represented by rows of stencilled white bombs. The overall scheme was 'tricolour blue', with the squadron emblem rendered in black and white.

25

SBD-5 White 207 of VMSB-236, flown by Lt Leo R Schall, Solomon Islands, late 1944

VMSB-236 flew the first dive-bombing attack on Bougainville in September 1943, and subsequently operated from Munda and Torokina, before moving to the Philippines in January 1945. the unit Participated in the Luzon and Mindanao campaigns, before being disestablished on 1 August. Besides the number on the nose and tail, SBD's of VMSB-236 could also be identified by a red prop spinner.

26

SBD-2 BuNo 2106 White 6 of VMSB-241, flown by 2nd Lt Daniel Iverson and PFC Wallace J Reid, Midway Atoll, 4 June 1942

This aircraft had previously flown in Bombing Two aboard *Lexington* from December 1941 to April 1942. Reassigned to VMSB-241, its prior markings were hastily obscured – the 'B' was painted out ahead of the number on the fuselage, and a thin coat of Blue-Grey was spread over the horizontal stripes on the rudder. Similarly, the red 'meatball' in the centre of the star was given a quick coat of white. Iverson brought the badly shot-up Dauntless back to Midway following an unsuccessful attack on the Japanese carriers.

27

SBD-5 White 12 of VMSB-331, Majuro Atoll, June 1944

Marine Corps squadrons frequently drew aircraft from an air group maintenance pool, resulting in occasionally contradictory markings. This Dauntless in the Marshall Islands is a case in point, with the previous unit number 26 being blanked out by dark grey paint applied to the vertical tail surfaces. The white 12 applied ahead of the fuselage national emblem was presumably the 'permanent' number intended for this aircraft, which flew anti-submarine patrols.

28

SBD-5 NZ5056 (BuNo 36924) White 56 of No 25 Sqn, RNZAF, flown by Flt Sgt C N O'Neill and Gunner Flt Sgt D W Gray, Piva Field, Solomons, April 1944

As the only dive-bombing unit within the RNZAF, No 25 Sqn was established in July 1943 using excess US Marine Corps aircraft. After an extensive work-up cycle on SBD-3s and -4s, the squadron drew new 'dash fives' and operated from Piva Field, on Bougainville, between March and May 1944. This particular aircraft saw much action with its assigned crew (each aircraft was allocated to a designated crew) in April/May 1944, pilot O'Neill single-handedly destroying a petrol dump at Rataval with a direct bomb hit on 6 May. NZ5056 was amongst the final trio of Dauntlesses returned to the USMC at Renards Field, in the Russell Islands, on 20 May 1944. Various markings and colour schemes were applied to the RNZAF SBDs, and unlike US Navy and Marine Corps examples, most of the Kiwi Dauntlesses in the frontline wore personalised emblems in the form of both artwork and names – this aircraft was later christened *'Paddy's Mistake'* and decorated with the bust of a 'blonde' below the cockpit on the port side. The SBDs used by the unit in the frontline all preserved their Marine Corps scheme, although evidence exists that some 'Kiwi' Dauntlesses in New Zealand flew with two-tone brown and green upper surfaces.

29

SBD-5 of *Flotille* **4FB,** *Aeronautique Navale,* **southern France, late 1944**

The French Navy operated two *flotilles* (squadrons) under *Groupe de Aeronavale* 2. Nos 3FB and 4FB were established in Morocco in late 1944 and were ready for combat by December. Retaining standard American Navy colour schemes, they applied their own national insignia in the form of cockades and fin flashes, with the addition of a black anchor. After the war they operated briefly from the light carrier *Arromanches.*

30

A-24B of Groupe de Combat I/18 'Vendee,' France, late 1944

This olive drab over grey Banshee belonged to the *Armeé de l'Air's* GC I/18, which was formed in Syria and Morocco during 1943 and committed to combat following the invasion of southern France in August 1944. Operations were conducted against defended cities such as Toulouse, Lorient and Bordeaux, with occasional missions against German-controlled coastal shipping too.

FIGURE PLATES

1

Maj Elmer G 'Iron Man' Glidden, CO of VMSB-231, Majuro Atoll (Central Pacific), June 1944. As the most experienced dive-bomber pilot in the US armed forces, Glidden is depicted wearing typical flying apparel as worn by SBD pilots and air gunners in either the US Navy or Marine Corps in the last two years of the Pacific war. His khaki flying coveralls come complete with lower leg pockets, over which he is wearing an early-issue life-preserver which harks back to his Midway and Guadalcanal days – note the dye marker attached to the lower left side of the vest, which has been added since the preserver was issued to its wearer. Glidden's seat-type parachute is also of relatively early-issue, lacking the additional leg straps associated with late-war 'chutes. His helmet appears to be a British Type C which may have been acquired in a trade with a RNZAF Kittyhawk, Corsair or Dauntless pilot met at one of the island airstrips. The major's goggles are US-issue B-7s, however, as are his QMC-issue 'Boondockers' on his feet.

2

Lt James M 'Moe' Vose, VB-8, USS *Hornet* (CV 8), Solomon Islands, October 1942. He is wearing standard issue US Navy officer's khaki shirt, trousers and matching belt, with rank tabs affixed to his shirt collars. Note the small survival knife in its leather scabbard hooked to the belt. Like Glidden, Vose wears a pre-war life-preserver, although his has no additional safety features. The lieutenant's helmet is one of the original tropical AN-H-15s issued to fleet pilots in mid-1942, and it is paired with AN-6530, or just simply B-7, goggles. His shoes are highly-polished black leather lace-ups (no 'Boondockers' aboard ship in those days!), and his gloves standard flying issue.

3

Lt James D 'Jig Dog' Ramage, VB-10, USS *Enterprise* (CV 6), Central Pacific, late 1943. Like 'Moe' Vose, Ramage is clothed in the standard officer's khaki shirt and trousers. However, his life-preserver has an additional dye marker pouch attached, and his footwear consists of QMC-issue 'Boondockers'. Although Ramage's helmet is basically an AN-H-15, it appears to have large earphone cups. Finally, his goggles are of the ubiquitous B-7 variety.

BIBLIOGRAPHY

Boggs, Charles W. *Marine Aviation in the Philippines.* Washington, DC, 1951

Buell, Harold. *Dauntless Helldivers.* New York, Orion, 1988

Cressman, Robert J, et al. *"A Glorious Page in Our History" The Battle of Midway.* Missoula, Pictorial Histories, 1990

Cressman, Robert J and J M Wenger. *"Steady Hands and Stout Hearts".* The Hook, August 1990

Cuny, J. *"Dauntlesses in French Service".* AAHS *Journal,* Spring 1967

Heinl, Robert D, Jr. *Marines at Midway.* USMC, 1948

Jenks, Cliff F L. *"Dive Bomber: The Douglas Dauntless in Royal New Zealand Air Force Service".* AAHS *Journal,* Spring 1972

Lambert, Jack. *Wildcats Over Casablanca.* Phalanx Publishing Co. Ltd., St. Paul, MN, 1992

Larkins, W T. *US Navy Aircraft 1921-1941 and U.S. Marine Corps Aircraft 1914-1959.* New York, Orion Books, 1988

Olynyk, Frank J. *USMC Credits for Destruction of Enemy Aircraft in Air-to-Air Combat, WW 2.* Privately published 1979

USN Credits for Destruction of Enemy Aircraft in Air-to-Air Combat, WW 2. Privately published 1982

Pattie, Donald A. *To Cock a Cannon: a Pilot's View of World War II.* Privately published 1983

Ramage, James D. *"A Review of the Philippine Sea Battle" The Hook,* August 1990

Sherrod, Robert. *History of Marine Corps Aviation in World War II.* Washington, DC; Combat Forces Press, 1952

Sakaida Henry. *Winged Samurai: Saburo Sakai and the Zero Fighter Pilots.* Mesa, AZ, Champlin Museum Press, 1985

Tillman, Barrett. *The Dauntless Dive Bomber of World War II.* Annapolis, Naval Institute Press, 1976

US Navy. *Monthly Location and Allowance of Aircraft,* 1941-1945

Van Vleet, Clarke. *"The First Carrier Raids" The Hook,* Winter 1978

White, Alexander. *Dauntless Marine: Joseph Sailer, Jr.* Fairfax Station, VA, White Knight Press, 1996